THE LOST
LEMON MINE

THE LOST LEMON MINE

An Unsolved Mystery of the Old West

RON STEWART

VICTORIA · VANCOUVER · CALGARY

Heritage House Publishing Company Ltd.
heritagehouse.ca

Library and Archives Canada Cataloguing in Publication
Stewart, Ron, 1951–
The Lost Lemon Mine: an unsolved mystery of the old West / Ron Stewart.

(Amazing stories)
Includes bibliographical references and index.
Issued also in electronic format.
ISBN 978-1-926613-99-4

1. Lost Lemon Mine (Alta.). 2. Gold miners—Crowsnest Pass Region (Alta. and B.C.). 3. Gold mines and mining—Crowsnest Pass Region (Alta. and B.C.). 4. Treasure troves—Crowsnest Pass Region (Alta. and B.C.). 5. Crowsnest Pass Region (Alta. and B.C.)—History. I. Title. II. Series: Amazing stories (Surrey, B.C.)

FC3661.8.S755 2011   971.23'4   C2011-900357-0

Series editor: Lesley Reynolds.
Proofreader: Liesbeth Leatherbarrow.
Cover design: Chyla Cardinal. Interior design: Frances Hunter.
Cover photo: Ron Stewart.

 The interior of this book was printed on 100% post-consumer recycled paper, processed chlorine free and printed with vegetable-based inks.

Heritage House acknowledges the financial support for its publishing program from the Government of Canada through the Canada Book Fund (CBF), Canada Council for the Arts and the province of British Columbia through the British Columbia Arts Council and the Book Publishing Tax Credit.

15 14 13   2 3 4 5
Printed in Canada

Contents

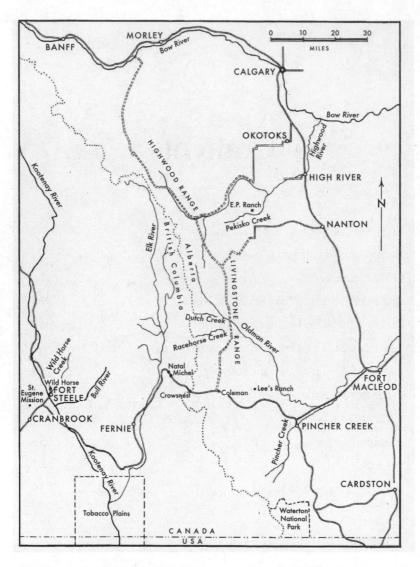

Southeastern British Columbia and southwestern Alberta, showing places significant to the Lost Lemon Mine story.

ADAPTED FROM A MAP DRAWN BY A.E. KNOX

Author's Note

SOLVING A HISTORICAL MYSTERY FROM fragmentary evidence that has survived for more than a century and a half is a daunting task. Many of the sources of the Lost Lemon Mine stories are little more than small, clipped fragments of old newspapers and periodicals—similar to the recipes your grandmother clipped and pasted in her scrapbook. The essential recipe is preserved, but often the source and date of publication are unknown.

Pinpointing the locations of events mentioned in these accounts is also difficult and, in some cases, impossible. Many place names have changed over the last 150 years. In 1870, the local name of a particular spot may have been Buffalo Wallow Creek, but as there have been no buffalo on the prairies for more than 100 years, no one alive today would know that Willow Creek and Buffalo Wallow Creek are, in fact, the same place.

Even the names of people vary with the storyteller. A prospector might have been known as Dancing Bill in one town, but if he left in a hurry after holding up the local bank, he might have called himself Yeastcake Will in the next town. There is no way of knowing if names that seem to indicate two individuals actually refer to one person.

For a better understanding of this complex mystery, I have taken several liberties to impose some order on the narrative. In most cases, I have standardized the spelling of the names of the central characters for clarity, for the author of each account seems to use a different spelling. References to First Nations people have been left in their original form in quoted material in order to preserve the accuracy and flavour of the historical account, and I intend no disrespect.

Prologue

A FORTUNE IN GOLD! *Lemon looked at the sleeping form of his prospecting partner, Blackjack. Sitting alone in the darkness and staring into the blazing campfire made a man think about his situation in life. For years he had endured the numbing winters, the blackflies and mosquitoes, eaten rotten grub and slept in wet clothes. It was more than any man should have to endure. Now here it was, finally within his grasp, a fortune in gold, warm beds, women—the life he had always dreamed of. The more he thought of it, the more he wondered why he should share all this bounty with Blackjack. It was true that they had a valid grubstake agreement filed with a trader, so if he tried to cut ol' Blackjack out of the game, it was sure to go badly for him. Folks had been strung up for welshing on an agreement. But still . . .*

The longer he gazed into the fire and watched the sparks ascend into the darkness of the black spruce, the surer he was of what he had to do. Silently, he made his way to the heavy axe, conveniently hacked into a nearby spruce stump. This would be much simpler than trying to negotiate with Blackjack, who was quick to take offence and blazing fast with his gun.

Raising the heavy axe, he looked at the slumbering man one more time. This was no time to change his mind. Swinging the steel with all his strength, he buried the axe's head in Blackjack's skull, snuffing out his life in an instant.

Relieved now that the deed was done, Lemon sat back down by the fire and smiled to himself. "They say gold does strange things to a man," he told Blackjack's corpse. "Yessirree, they do say that."

Introduction

THE LEGEND OF THE Lost Lemon Mine has all the requisite ingredients of every great story of the Old West: murder, massacres, gunfighters, bushwhackers and a fortune in gold lost for over a century. Given the mass appeal of hidden treasures and unsolved mysteries, it is hardly surprising that the Lost Lemon Mine has been the subject of so much speculation. Many short stories and articles about the mine have appeared over the last 140 years, but while these accounts make for interesting reading, sadly none tell the complete story.

Not surprisingly, the stories that have survived the years are twisted, confused and convoluted. Told and retold around countless campfires, the tales of the Lost Lemon Mine took on a life of their own. No longer bound by the constraints of fact or circumstance, each account has undergone a subtle metamorphosis with each telling, emerging as part of the folklore that survives today.

The Lost Lemon Mine stories may be grouped into several categories. The best-known of the narratives—those usually seen in print—are prospector stories that tell of Lemon and his partner discovering gold somewhere in the Rocky Mountains, usually in a pit or mine. Another group of tales presents a much darker picture of the mysterious Lemon, describing murder and robbery on the lonely trails of the goldfields. These desperado narratives are largely unknown to the reading public and over the last century have languished in private collections and historical archives of the West. A third group focuses on the Native people: it seems that the same individuals are mentioned again and again in every version of the Lost Lemon Mine story. These tales tell of stolen gold and of a Stoney boy who became obsessed with Lemon's treasure over a century ago and spent most of his life searching for the lost Eldorado. Rounding out the available material on the Lost Lemon Mine is biographical information concerning Lemon and other characters in this historical puzzle.

The mystery of the Lost Lemon Mine was born in the frontier goldfields. Its principal characters, the enigmatic Lemon and Blackjack, were typical of the prospectors who struggled against the wilderness, bone-numbing cold, starvation and each other in their quest for golden wealth. While many locations have been suggested as the possible site of the Lost Lemon Mine, several accounts seem to point toward the goldfields located on Wild Horse Creek, near Fort Steele, BC.

The Wild Horse Creek gold rush began in 1864, following Joe Finlay's discovery of gold in a small stream about 50 miles north of the British Columbia–Montana border in the fall of 1863. This stream, a tributary of the Kootenay River, is known today as Finlay Creek. Word of the gold strike spread into the United States when Finlay showed his golden nuggets to John "Scotty" Linklater, the trader at the Tobacco Plains, Montana, trading post. The news soon filtered through the smoky dance halls and mining camps south of the border, and miners headed north to take their chances in the new gold rush.

Two parties of prospectors headed north of Finlay Creek to the junction of the Kootenay and St. Mary Rivers. Bob Dore, an Englishman leading a party of six men, was the first to get underway. A couple of days later, on March 17, 1864, Jack Fisher followed with a group of 15 prospectors. Neither group knew exactly where Finlay had made his strike, yet remarkably, after travelling through rugged country for 400 miles, both groups ended up camping on the same river only a few hundred yards apart. As the snow was still too deep to prospect in earnest, the miners passed the time panning for gold at a nearby creek.

Dore's group, working at the mouth of the creek, found colour (a miner's term for a speck of gold) but nothing spectacular. Meanwhile, Fisher and two of his men pushed on about five miles up a steep-sided canyon. When they reached a wide, flat gravel bar, they decided to test it. They shovelled out the gravel, panned it and were rewarded with large quantities of free gold.

When Fisher held up that first pan to show the gold to Pat Quirk and Ike Stevens, the men's yells and yahoos of delight echoed up and down the valley. The three were so excited that they shovelled and panned until dark, without even stopping to eat. So began the golden bonanza of Wild Horse Creek. Before it was over, an incredible 48 tons of the yellow metal were pulled from its frigid gravel.

The wealth that came out of some of the claims was staggering. The largest nugget found at Wild Horse Creek weighed 37 ounces and was pure gold. Bob Dore, using little more than a bowie knife and an axe, managed to fashion himself a crude wheelbarrow. Even with these primitive tools, with the help of four men he was able to take out $7,000 a day in gold—this at a time when the average wage for miners working in the damp and dirty mine shafts of the Cariboo was $8 to $10 per day. Dore's workings paid out more in a week than most men could earn in a lifetime. In three years, his company made $521,700.

There are two basic types of gold mining: hard-rock and placer. Hard-rock mining refers to underground techniques that remove gold found in vein deposits, frequently in veins

Introduction

of quartz. In British Columbia and the Yukon, gold is often found in association with quartz veins. Other minerals that may also contain gold are iron pyrites, commonly called "fool's gold," and an ore of lead called galena. Hard-rock mining usually requires specialized mining equipment and modern processing mills to separate gold from waste rock.

Placer-mining techniques were commonly used during the 19th-century British Columbia gold rushes. A placer (pronounced PLASS-er) is a deposit of sand or gravel containing particles of gold. When rocks containing gold erode, natural forces like frost, wind and water break up the material and carry it away. This sediment is carried into rivers and streams, and because gold is about 19 times denser than water, it sinks and settles. The settling tends to concentrate the gold in certain sand or gravel bars, and this sorting action of the streams makes placer mining possible.

In its basic form, placer mining is nothing more than a prospector panning for gold. A miner shovels gravel into the pan and then washes it by swirling the water around. This flushes out the light material, allowing the gold to settle to the bottom. While this sounds easy, in reality it is back-breaking work. Unless a miner had a lot of luck and found a rich piece of ground, he could shovel tons of gravel without finding even a speck of colour. In itself, a speck of colour may only be worth a hundredth part of a cent, but it is a clue that may indicate richer gravels just upstream or deeper in the sandbar.

These Chinese miners at Wild Horse Creek in the 1880s used streams of water under pressure to cut away banks of gold-bearing gravel or soil and wash it into a series of sluice boxes.
GLENBOW ARCHIVES NA-1455-7

Sometimes the gold-bearing gravels were buried under a layer of overburden, and a shaft had to be sunk. The simple mines that were dug to reach these gravels were little more than glorified holes. Using picks and shovels, with no ventilation and the ever-present danger of a cave-in, miners braved the mud and cold to reach the pay dirt. The gold-bearing gravel was hauled to the surface in baskets or ore cars and then washed using large sluice boxes. While these methods may seem primitive, they produced vast amounts of gold. The mines on Williams Creek in the Cariboo, of which the famous Neversweat is the best known, produced upwards of $25 million in gold.

The search for gold was not confined to the mountains of BC. After the American Civil War, large numbers of prospectors moved north across the border to try their luck in Alberta.

The discovery of gold in the gravels of the North Saskatchewan River at Fort Edmonton first brought miners into the region in the 1860s. When word of this strike filtered back to Montana, eager prospectors headed north in search of a bonanza. Unfortunately for these fortune seekers, Alberta's rivers yielded only extremely fine gold flakes, called flour gold, of which it would take several hundred to equal the value of a cent. This initial failure to strike it rich did little to discourage fortune hunters, however, and for many years prospectors scoured the gravels of Alberta's rivers.

The promise of rich placer deposits on the North Saskatchewan River may have brought Lemon and his partner, Blackjack, into the area around Fort Edmonton.

CHAPTER

1

The Prospector Stories

THE BEST-KNOWN STORIES ABOUT the Lost Lemon Mine focus on the discovery of rich gold diggings by a pair of prospectors—Lemon and his partner, Blackjack—and any investigation into the legend must begin with these accounts. While the details vary considerably, the prospector stories outline a tale of fabulous discovery, greed and murder.

Daniel E. Riley's Account

The following account is based upon the article "The Lost Lemon Mine," written by Senator Daniel E. Riley, which first appeared in *Alberta Folklore Quarterly* in March 1946. Senator Riley's tale is certainly the best known of all versions of the Lost Lemon Mine story and has been widely reprinted in newspaper and magazine articles. Variations of this story form the basis of most published articles about the Lost Lemon Mine.

Daniel Edward Riley was born in Baltic, Prince Edward Island. He taught school there for several years before moving west in 1882. In the fall of that year, he arrived in Winnipeg, stopping to work over the winter in the shops of the Canadian Pacific Railway (CPR). During this period he met an ex–US Cavalry man by the name of Bob Fennell, who had spent many years as an Indian fighter and frontiersman. Fennell told such outlandish yarns about the Wild West that he inspired young Riley to head west with him the following spring. Their destination was a place the Blackfoot called Spitzee Post, near present-day High River, Alberta.

Reaching the South Saskatchewan River at Medicine Hat, they made their way to Blackfoot Crossing on the Bow River. The following day, on their arrival at the crossing, Dan Riley first met rancher George Emmerson and Lafayette French, a trader, prospector and cattleman who plays a large role in many versions of the Lost Lemon Mine story. Riley worked for French off and on for several years. In 1883 and 1884, French grubstaked the Natives who had travelled with Lemon and Blackjack, and it was probably during this time that Riley first heard the story of the Lost Lemon Mine from French.

During French's later years, Riley was always ready to grubstake his old friend, and he would even join him on many trips deep into the back country, searching for the lost mine. It was certainly as a result of these trips and the outlandish tales he heard from French that Riley formed his keen interest in the Lost Lemon Mine, a preoccupation that would continue for the remainder of his life.

Riley later entered politics and in 1906 became mayor of High River. By 1925, he had been appointed to the Canadian Senate. Senator Riley died in April 1948. Two years before his death, he wrote the following account of the Lost Lemon Mine.

In the spring of 1870, a party of prospectors left Tobacco Plains, heading north to search the gravels of the North Saskatchewan River for gold. Among this party were two men staked by an old-time trader and buffalo hunter named Lafayette French. The men were Lemon and his partner, Blackjack, who was reputed to be the best prospector in the West and the true discoverer of the Cariboo goldfields in BC.

Later that year, having had little success on the North Saskatchewan, Lemon and Blackjack decided to leave the party and travel south with a band of Metis led by a man named La Nouse. Due to raids by hostile Blackfoot, this arrangement was much safer than travelling alone on the dangerous trek south.

After a time, the group split up. La Nouse and his band travelled south toward Fort Standoff, a notorious whisky fort situated at the junction of the Kootenay and Belly rivers, while Lemon and Blackjack followed an old First Nations lodgepole trail that led up the High River toward Tobacco Plains. As they travelled, they prospected the river gravels, finding good showings of placer gold. Following the mountain stream toward its headwaters, they stumbled upon rich diggings with placer gold scattered from grassroots to bedrock. Stopping to investigate this find, they excavated two pits, and while bringing in their horses from the picket line, they accidentally discovered the ledge from which the gold had come. The samples collected from this ledge were described by traders at Fort Benton as indescribably rich— essentially lumps of solid gold with a little rock running through them.

Late that night, the magnitude of the find led to a heated argument between Lemon and Blackjack. Although we will never know what was said around that campfire, according to Lemon, they could not agree on whether to stake the find and return in the spring or simply set up camp on the site and protect their bonanza. Whatever decision the partners reached, Lemon decided to take matters into his own hands. Waiting until Blackjack was asleep, rolled up in his blankets, he crept up on his slumbering partner, hoisted a bush axe above his head and smashed the sleeping man's skull.

Overwhelmed by the horror of his crime, Lemon was seized with panic. Surrounded on all sides by the darkness and confronted with Blackjack's shattered body, he built a huge fire and kept vigil beside the blazing logs. Haunted by his fears and with his gun at the ready, Lemon paced about the small circle of light like a caged animal, waiting for dawn.

Little did Lemon know that his savage deed had been witnessed by William and Daniel Bendow, two Stoney braves who had been following the pair for some time and had observed the sinking of the pits and their discovery of gold. As he huddled by the fire, Lemon's distress was apparent to these young men, and it must have been some grim sense of humour that compelled them to compound Lemon's fears by making strange moaning sounds in the darkness. There can be little doubt that this torment contributed to the madness that later afflicted Lemon.

With the coming of first light, Lemon saddled his pony and headed off through the mountains to Tobacco Plains. The two Stoney braves then ransacked the camp, taking the remaining horses to their village at Morley, where they related their strange story to Chief Jacob Bearspaw. Fearful of a gold rush and an influx of white men overrunning the Stoney hunting grounds, Chief Bearspaw swore the two young braves to everlasting secrecy.

When Lemon arrived in Tobacco Plains, he confessed his crime to an old friend, a priest. As Lemon told his wild tale to the priest, he showed him the gold he and Blackjack had collected from their bonanza. At times Lemon rambled on, half-crazed with the recollection of his hideous deed. Wasting no time, the priest dispatched John McDougall, a

Metis mountain man, to the scene of the murder to investigate the strange tragedy. McDougall found Blackjack's body and buried him, erecting a mound of stones on the grave to protect the corpse from prowling animals. He then returned to Tobacco Plains to tell his story to the priest. But McDougall had been watched from the forest by a group of Stoneys, and as soon as he left the scene, Bearspaw's braves scattered the stones from the grave and obliterated all trace of the murder and the camp. They must have done their work very well, for this ground has never revealed its dark secret. Over the winter, Lemon remained in Tobacco Plains, drifting in and out of madness, comforted only by the priest. Like all gold finds, there seemed little hope that this one could be kept secret, and soon word of Lemon's strike had spread far afield. With the coming of spring, a large group of prospectors, led by Lemon, set out to relocate the bonanza.

But the fates were against them. Although Lemon scoured the coulees and hillsides, he could not relocate the fabulous strike. One can only imagine the mood of the men, filled with gold fever, who followed Lemon. It would have taken little more than mutterings to convince them that Lemon was deliberately misleading them, no doubt hoping to slink back later and stake the claim himself. It is almost certain that Lemon was threatened with death at the hands of this mob for failing to reveal the location of the bonanza. The confrontation with the miners certainly caused Lemon to relapse into madness, and he became violently insane. Perhaps thinking that Lemon's madness was feigned and that he was waiting for an opportunity to slip away, the prospectors placed him under guard. The next morning, Lemon was escorted back to Tobacco Plains.

The following year, another party set out from Tobacco Plains. Outfitted by the priest, the expedition was to be led by John McDougall, the man who had buried Blackjack. McDougall, who was at Fort Benton, Montana, agreed to rendezvous with the rest of the party at Crowsnest Lake. From there, he would lead them north to the murder scene.

Again the fates conspired to keep the gold secreted beneath the dark mountains. Other than the Stoney braves, McDougall was the only man who had been to the scene of the murder, and the group badly needed his guidance. As agreed, McDougall had left Fort Benton to keep his rendezvous at Crowsnest Lake, but he had stopped en route at Fort Kipp, a notorious whisky fort. Fort Kipp was set up for the purpose of separating Native people from their furs for as little cost as possible, and whisky made the fort very profitable.

Trade whisky was made from all manner of ingredients, but a typical recipe was one gallon of wine, three gallons of water, one quart of alcohol, one pound of rank chewing tobacco, one handful of red peppers, one bottle of Jamaica ginger and one quart of black molasses. This mixture was stirred well and then boiled until all the strength was drawn from the tobacco and peppers.

This vile concoction, also known as "rotgut," was incredibly potent, and whoever drank it simply went wild and sometimes died from its effects. But it was an inexpensive and very profitable commodity for the whisky traders. Unfortunately for the prospectors at Crowsnest Lake, McDougall drank too much rotgut whisky; he was buried at Fort Kipp, along with a vital clue to the secret of the Lost Lemon Mine.

The next year, another prospecting party was organized from Tobacco Plains, but it met with failure after reaching Crowsnest Lake. A fire had recently burned over the area, destroying the timber and, more important, the grass necessary to feed the horses. As a result, the party had to turn back to Tobacco Plains.

The following year, a smaller party was organized by the priest under the guidance of Lemon, who was still living at Tobacco Plains. As before, however, upon reaching the vicinity of the murder, Lemon became violently unstable, and the group was forced to return to Tobacco Plains empty-handed. Lemon never fully recovered his reason; he left Alberta and his lost mine, never to return, spending the remainder of his days with his brother on a ranch in Texas.

Having met with repeated failure, the priest gave up the search for Lemon's lost mine, but there was no shortage of others prepared to continue the quest. A man named Nelson, a member of the original Lemon party, took up the pursuit, organizing yet another expedition to hunt for the mine. When an exhaustive search failed to turn up any clues to the whereabouts of the mine, the party disbanded, leaving each member to conduct his own private exploration of the area. Like all other attempts, these too were doomed to failure.

Lafayette French, the outfitter who had originally staked Lemon and Blackjack, returned to Tobacco Plains determined to find the cache of hidden gold. He was struck by a strange sickness while searching the mountains and made his way back to Tobacco Plains more dead than alive. It seemed as if some strange curse had been placed upon those who searched for Lemon's blood-stained gold. French had a map in his possession, which he showed to a friend. It was a rough sketch of the mountains and streams. At the headwaters of a stream with three forks was an X and written beside it was the magical word "GOLD!" French claimed that the map had been drawn by Lemon, with the mark representing the location of the lost mine. Determined to search for Lemon's gold as long as he drew breath, French roamed the backcountry for the next 30 years, devoting himself to this quest.

In the winter of 1883, French furnished La Nouse and his band with enough supplies to keep them through the winter so that, in the spring, they could retrace the trip Blackjack and Lemon had made with the band in 1870. We have no way of knowing if they actually made this trip.

French spent much time pondering the details of the

earlier expeditions. In the 1890s, he spent several months with a pair of survivors from the original expedition led by Lemon. They carefully retraced their movements along the trail north from Crowsnest Lake, hoping to identify some landmarks in the country they had travelled with Lemon. We can assume that this search was unsuccessful.

No doubt French had hoped to learn the secret of Lemon's mine from William Bendow, one of the Stoney braves who had witnessed the murder of Blackjack. To this end, French fed Bendow and his band one winter at William Lee's ranch near Pincher Creek. In the spring, a deal was struck between French and the Stoneys. French placed 25 horses and 25 head of cattle in a pasture. This livestock would become Stoney property the moment that Bendow led French to the location of Blackjack's murder.

The second day out on the trail, a great fear came over Bendow. Perhaps he was afraid of breaking his promise to Chief Jacob Bearspaw and betraying his tribe to French, but whatever the cause, he refused to take another step toward the Lost Lemon Mine. Again, the expedition had to be called off.

Late in 1912, French made a last attempt to locate the Lost Lemon Mine. He had made a new deal with William Bendow to lead him to the place where Blackjack died. Bendow and his band of Stoneys were on their way to the reservation at Morley and had agreed to camp at the George Sage place, an abandoned ranch on the middle fork of the High River, until French could get his friend George Emmerson to join them. As before, Bendow had agreed to lead them to the murder site.

Once more, however, tragedy struck: William Bendow suddenly died during the night. Whatever the cause, the Stoneys took this as an unmistakable sign of bad medicine caused by Bendow's intention to betray the tribe's secret. The remaining Stoneys promptly left the area. They loaded Bendow's body on a Red River cart and returned it to the reserve at Morley. The night of their arrival, Bendow's son-in-law also died in a mysterious manner, another sure sign of bad medicine and of the wrath of Wahcondah—the Stoney Great Spirit. To this day, the Stoneys become tight-lipped and grim in response to inquiries regarding the Lost Lemon Mine.

Even French could not escape the apparent curse. On the night of his return from this last expedition, he was terribly burned in a mysterious fire that swept through the Emmerson house. On that very same evening, he had posted a letter to a friend in Fort Benton, Montana. Written in a state of extreme excitement, the note declared that French had located "it" and was coming to High River in a few days to enlist his friend's help and tell everything. Unfortunately, due to the injuries he suffered in the fire, French died around Christmas Day in 1912, taking his answers to the mystery of the Lost Lemon Mine to his grave.

Freda Bundy's Account

The second of the prospector stories dealing with the Lost Lemon Mine is based upon the writings of Freda Bundy, a pioneer newspaperwoman and historian. Elfreda Graham Bundy was born in 1895 in Truro, Nova Scotia. She graduated from the Nova Scotia Provincial Normal School in 1914 and moved west to begin teaching at Lethbridge, Alberta. Freda married Clarence J. Bundy in 1916, and they had three children. In the 1920s, she began writing feature articles for various newspapers and periodicals, most notably the *Lethbridge Herald* and the *Pincher Creek Echo*. During her long career as an author, she wrote many articles and plays, as well as an autobiography entitled *Go West Young Woman*. Freda and Clarence retired to Pincher Creek, where she died in 1962.

The following account is based upon Bundy's article concerning the Lost Lemon Mine, which appeared in the *Family Herald and Weekly Star* on March 9, 1938. Bundy was familiar with many stories of the Old West, but none, she claimed, were more colourful or exaggerated than the story of the Lost Lemon Mine, or the Lemon Diggings, as she says the pioneers around Pincher Creek called it. Most of these pioneers could tell a version of this old tale, but they didn't agree upon the exact details of what happened.

Although Bundy admitted that it was very difficult to say whether or not the story was true, she said that old Gladstone, the first white settler in the area, knew about the mine and was a valuable source of information. It seems certain that he and other pioneers, like Bill Olin, Matt Holloway and John Nelson, believed in the existence of the Lost Lemon Mine; they would hardly have spent so many years searching the mountains for the gold had they doubted the truth of the original story.

A man named Garifel, who was an early prospector of the Cariboo gold rush, thought the gold must be on the British Columbia side of the border. He spent his time prospecting along the Bull River beyond St. Eugene Mission. It has been suggested that Lemon's gold came from this part of the country. Some of the stories told by the early settlers concern a sack of gold that Lemon obtained from First Nations people, possibly in the area of Fort Steele, in exchange for horses and other trade goods he and Blackjack had brought in from Montana.

While the account of the Lost Lemon Mine is certainly colourful and romantic, Bundy concluded that the facts concerning its exact location were exceedingly controversial. Lemon himself told many versions of the story, and each pioneer who retold the tale claims to have heard it directly from Lemon himself. Over the years, there have been a number of mini-rushes, each in an area rumoured to be the hiding place of Lemon's gold. In 1931, and again in 1933, there was a rush southwest of Nanton and High River, but it fizzled out when nothing was found. Other pioneers have always maintained that the true location of the Lost Lemon

Mine is in the vicinity of Crowsnest Lake or along the upper reaches of Racehorse Creek.

There is an old First Nations pack trail running along Racehorse Creek and over the Racehorse Pass that Lemon, Bill Olin and John Nelson used to cross the mountains into British Columbia on their way to an early mission. Bundy suggested a possible connection between the trail and Lemon's lost gold. She based this on a story Bill Olin told in Pincher Creek and vicinity. According to Bundy, a short time after the North West Mounted Police (NWMP) established Fort Macleod in 1873, two prospectors drifted into the barracks from Montana. There had been rumours of gold finds on the North Saskatchewan River at Fort Edmonton, and Bill Lemon and his partner, Jim, had travelled up the Whoop-Up Trail from Fort Benton to try their luck. The Mounties at Fort Macleod knew there was not much gold to be found in that country and tried without success to convince Lemon and Jim to abandon their trip north to Fort Edmonton. Lemon and his partner shrugged off the good advice and headed north anyway. Members of the force from the early days remembered Lemon and his partner and the wild yarns Lemon told about his "lost mine." In the months that followed, police riders frequently encountered the two prospectors washing for gold in many of the mountain streams. It was never known exactly where Lemon and his partner got their gold. They may have found a vein near the mouth of Racehorse Creek or washed it out of the streams on the eastern side of the mountains. Some have suggested they may have travelled over the divide into British Columbia and made their strike as far west as St. Eugene Mission. This area is extremely rich in placer gold and certainly seems a possible source of Lemon's gold, whether it was obtained by panning or in trade with First Nations people.

Lemon and his partner built a crude cabin in the north country and prospected there for some time. According to the policemen who knew them, Lemon seems to have been an educated adventurer, while his partner was an uncouth ruffian. Exactly what happened between Lemon and Jim will never be known, but an old-time trader and buffalo hunter named John Nelson learned some of the details from a First Nations man he met on his travels who wished to trade gold nuggets for rum. When he saw the gold, Nelson began to question the man at gunpoint. Wisely answering Nelson's questions, the man said that he had encountered a prospector riding alone on the trail that ran from the north country to Fort Benton and had bushwhacked and murdered the miner for his poke.

Nelson lost no time in sharing this information with his friends Bill Olin and Matt Holloway, two old-time buffalo hunters who had come north with him from Montana and had settled at La Grandeur's Crossing on the Oldman River. Bill Olin, William Lee and a trapper by the name of Biggs set out into the north country. The trail took them past the Whispering Gates of the North Fork and farther back into the mountains until they found Lemon's cabin. In the abandoned shanty, they found Lemon's corpse. Apparently he had been killed the winter before. Along with the body, they found a note penned by Lemon, accusing Jim of wounding him and leaving him for dead. Lemon had cursed his partner and said that Jim would most likely be heading south along the trail to Fort Benton. He had written that he hoped whoever found his body might follow and bring his murderer to justice.

In later years, Olin said that he and his companions buried Lemon's remains in a nearby cave, since a proper burial was impossible because the ground was still frozen. A careful search of the cabin and surrounding area provided no clue to the source of the nuggets.

According to Freda Bundy's account, the First Nations man said that the lone rider he had met was Lemon's partner Jim, but just how he knew this is not made clear. The story does not mention the Native man's fate, but given John Nelson's apparently excitable nature, it's reasonable to assume that his prospects were less than bright, especially after he had admitted murdering a white miner.

And what of Lemon's gold? According to Freda Bundy:

This story spread like a prairie fire over the south and the buffalo hunters and prospectors drifted up the Racehorse Creek, hoping to find a blazed trail or location of some sort, marking the whereabouts of the famous "Lemon Diggings," but neither trail, nugget or gold dust was ever found on the eastern slope of the Divide and it was not for lack of seekers and explorers.

Down the years, the story has persisted with many variations, supposedly authentic maps have cropped up at times but later proved to be false clues, and many an early settler and raw cowhand were inveigled into parting with their bit of earthly wealth by some smooth talker who declared that he had the secret location from information that Lemon had left.

The Original Newspaper Stories

Only two original stories relating to Lemon and his gold are found in the newspapers of the day. While they differ from all other surviving accounts of the story, they may in fact reveal the truth about the Lost Lemon Mine. Perhaps what we have been seeing for over 100 years is merely a phantom born of rumours of gold and stories clipped from faded newspapers.

Settle back and try to imagine that you are a newspaper reader in the summer of 1870. This account appeared in the *Helena Daily Rocky Mountain Gazette* on August 6, 1870:

THE STAMPEDE TO THE FLATHEAD COUNTRY
Its Causes and Consequences

About the 28th day of June, 1870, Frank Lemmon, a blacksmith at the mouth of Cedar Creek, stated to Jeff Standifer (the-well known prospector who led a party into the Wind River country a few years ago), Ben Northington and others that he got as high as $15 or $20 to the pan in a gulch in the Blackfoot range of the Flathead country. He said: "Gentlemen, I have not been there in two years, my partner was killed by the Indians about eighteen miles from the diggings—shot by the Blackfeet." He also said that he lived on rose-buds and service berries until he reached the Jocko Mission. When he arrived at Helena, two years ago, he tried to induce parties to embark in the expedition, but they thinking it was a "bilk," the matter dropped until he arrived at Cedar a month or two ago.

In the later part of June, 1870, a party was organized at Cedar Creek to accompany Frank Lemmon to the new Eldorado. They appointed an old miner from Walla Walla, Captain, to pilot them through and proceeded on the journey 250 miles from Cedar Creek. After travelling 250 miles, the party appointed five men to go with Mr. Lemmon to the place where he reported the fabulous prospects. Nothing daunted, these hardy mountaineers proceeded to Lemmon's Creek, 120 miles from Flathead Lake. The originator of the stampede claimed this to be the creek and showed his followers two holes, caused by two trees having been torn up by the roots, and said these were the prospect holes sunk by him and his partner two years before. At this juncture Barnum asked Lemmon if he had ever been in this country before, or if he had ever got a prospect. Lemmon told him (crying at the same time) that he wanted to do the best he could for the boys. He also said that he thought he could find the holes four miles from there. For days, he led on his followers through a terrible rough country with no trail after leaving Grave Creek, ever and anon pointing out a tree or a mountain, stating that to be the locality of the new Flathead mines.

This party not finding the place after an extended

search, started back, to the main camp, Lemmon, the guide, getting lost did not arrive in camp for three days, when by accident he stumbled upon it. The party here had met with an accident, by a fire breaking out in camp which came near destroying themselves and animals. The flames went up hundreds of feet. Many became panic stricken, and the wildest excitement ensued. They only saved themselves and their horses by rushing into a swamp, which action was suggested by one of the party. If this prompt action had not been thought of and taken at the moment, nearly all would have perished, I am told, in the flames, certainly the animals. The party believing themselves "bilked" commenced prospecting on what they supposed to be the middle fork of the Flathead River, getting from five to twenty cents to the pan, but did not reach bedrock. They were about out of grub, and 250 miles from where supplies could be obtained, therefore they had to forego prospecting further and turn their steps homeward, and arrived on the 28th day of June 1870, after weeks of travel in an unprospected and underdeveloped country, many of them dead broke and now with the mining season far advanced, to commence anew to recuperate their lost fortunes. About ten of the party intend going back to "prospect" as soon as they can recruit up a little. Although this was a wild and unremunerative stampede it may be the cause, in the course of a short time, of opening up a new country to the miner and ranchman unparalleled in richness. I was told that here was no better grazing country, and all that is needed is to develop the mines. Although this company of prospectors had been misled and misinformed, I heard none speak disparagingly of the Flathead country.

H.C.W.

The second original newspaper account seems to contain elements of the Lost Lemon Mine story that appear in most versions of the tale. It appeared in the *Calgary Daily Herald* on Saturday, October 6, 1886.

THE LEMON GULCH

A week or two ago a party of prospectors started out to renew the search for what is known as the Lemon Gulch. As many vague stories are in circulation about this old-time find, it may not be out of place to give the real history of it.

Lemon was a prospector who came up north into this country within a hundred miles of Edmonton in '64. He was with a party of thirty or forty others who had been attracted from Montana by the news of successful digging on the Saskatchewan. About 75 miles south of Edmonton, the Montana outfit and another party coming from that place decided to try their luck in the newly discovered diggings at Virginia City and Buhnock City. Lemon and his partner, who went by the name of "Old George" and who was a man of a morose and surly character, turned down south again with the Edmonton crowd and accompanied them as far as the mouth of Pine Coulee in the Porcupines. At this point the two of them struck off from the main body and went into the mountains hoping to discover a pass which would take them to the Kootenai diggings, the fame of which was also beginning to be noised abroad at that time. They struck either the Crow's Nest or the pass now called the North Kootenai, just south of it, and plunged into the mountains. Exactly what happened there has never been known. At any rate Lemon turned up in Missoula Montana, with a story of the discovery of a good prospect somewhere on the Red Deer River in British Columbia, a stream which has nothing to do with our Red Deer, which at that time was universally known as the Elk River. He was also without his partner, whom he owned to having shot in some quarrel, the cause of which was unexplained. A party of three other miners agreed to go back with him and try to refind the spot, where he had discovered these rich indications. Another outfit of about twenty followed them in a small "stampede." On getting back into the mountains Lemon could not find the exact place and could only indicate a certain part of the country, over which his party began to prospect. The others thinking Lemon was trying to fool them got hostile and proposed to hang him for misleading them. The feeling against him got so strong that his friends put him on his horse and started him off back in the night, returning later without success.

Lemon has we believe been seen at the new diggings in the Sweet Grass Hills recently. The body of his partner was found and buried a year or two ago.

This is the story of the Lemon gulch which has sufficed to keep the spark of hope alive in the hearts of prospectors for over twenty years, although he never pretended to have discovered anything but good indications. As we stated before, there is a party engaged in an attempt to rediscover them at the present time and has been all summer.

Ay-Ko-Skun and the Lost Lemon Mine

The final Lost Lemon prospector story is certainly the least well known. It is based upon a fascinating tale that appeared in the *Lethbridge Herald* on January 5, 1960. The newspaper article, entitled "Ay-Ko-Skun and the Lost Lemon Mine," was written by a woman named Florence Kroesing.

Florence Kroesing (née Gladstone) was born in 1895 and lived in the Pincher Creek area. She was married in 1915 to Ernest Kroesing and settled in Coleman prior to 1924. She seems to have lived her entire life in the Crowsnest Pass, where she raised a family of four daughters and two sons. It was reported that Florence Kroesing was an excellent midwife, having first assisted in the delivery of a baby when she was only 12 years old. Over the years she helped at the births of many residents of the Crowsnest Pass. Mrs. Kroesing had a remarkable knowledge of Native medicine and herbal cures, a gift she attributed to her Plains Cree heritage. In the 1960s, Mrs. Kroesing put her pen to paper and wrote many historical articles dealing with the early days and Native folklore. Several of her stories were published and used by the CBC.

Florence Kroesing's mother obtained knowledge of the Lost Lemon Mine as a result of caring for a Blood woman named Ay-Ko-Skun and her 11-year-old son. Ay-Ko-Skun claimed to have been with Lemon and his partner during their trip to the mine. It was very common for prospectors and trappers to have Native wives. Other than the obvious benefits of companionship, these marriages took advantage of the Native concept of extended family. A prospector married to a Native wife could travel through her tribe's territory without fear of attack.

What follows is based upon Florence Kroesing's 1960 newspaper article, which contains information regarding Ay-Ko-Skun's travels that may help us to unravel the mystery of the location of the Lost Lemon Mine.

The story began on the Blood Reserve near Cardston, Alberta, when Jack Lemmon (Kroesing's spelling) and his partner rode in to purchase supplies for a trip into the mountains. However, it seems that in addition to purchasing moccasins and pemmican, Lemmon also bought a wife. Ay-Ko-Skun, or Cloud Walker, a widow with a small son of 11 years, was obtained in trade for two horses and a Hudson's Bay Company (HBC) blanket. The chief of the Bloods performed a marriage ceremony, and Lemmon and Ay-Ko-Skun became man and wife according to Blood custom.

There was a law in effect in those days that no white man was allowed to remain on the reserve after sundown, so Lemmon and his party left to camp up the river. The next day, they went by way of Lee's Lake, with Ay-Ko-Skun's young son riding a pinto pony and Lemmon, his partner and Ay-Ko-Skun each leading a pack horse. They continued their trip until darkness overtook them.

The country was extremely wild. Making few stops, they made their way into the Livingstone Range. Following little more than First Nations game trails, they wound their way deeper into the wilderness. At the foot of a low mountain, they came to a small clearing in the bush, where an unfinished cabin stood. After Ay-Ko-Skun prepared a traditional meal of bannock and pemmican for Lemmon and his partner, she put up her painted teepee and her young son's buckskin tent, where they were to sleep. Lemmon and his partner slept in the cabin, where the food supplies were stored.

There was much for Ay-Ko-Skun to do, and with the help of her son she chopped and packed firewood, smoked any deer meat that Lemmon brought back to camp and performed all the cooking and camp duties. When there was time, she also sewed moccasins and other clothing for the miners.

Lemmon had dug a hole in the floor of the small cabin to hide his cache of gold. Each morning he would show Ay-Ko-Skun the buckskin poke that contained the dust; then he would return the gold to his secret place and cover the hole with a buckskin water bag. Ay-Ko-Skun said that in the late spring, when food was running low, she was told to round up the horses. She built an enclosure from poles and brush and put the three horses she had captured into the corral. Later that evening, Lemmon went over the small rise to look at the livestock.

Once Lemmon was out of sight, his partner went to the cabin, took the rifle and headed off into the bush after him. Several minutes later, Ay-Ko-Skun heard a shot from the darkness. Then all was silent.

A short time later, Lemmon's partner returned alone and demanded his supper. He also wanted Ay-Ko-Skun to boil up the rest of the deer meat and pack it with the bannock. He said he planned to leave early in the morning and that Ay-Ko-Skun and her son should wait until his return. Fearing the worst, Ay-Ko-Skun glanced off into the dark trees toward the horse corral. Her husband still had not returned. "He's not coming back," Lemmon's partner said as he hit Ay-Ko-Skun across the face. Then, after he had finished his meal, he ransacked the cabin looking for the hidden gold.

Fearing for the safety of her young son, Ay-Ko-Skun told the boy to take a plate of food and a blanket from his tent and hide in the bush until she called for him the next day. Only when he was safely out of sight did she return to her teepee. Taking a blanket to ward off the night chill, she sought refuge under a rock ledge near the creek. Ay-Ko-Skun could hear the miner calling her in the darkness until well after midnight. Much later that night, she summoned up enough courage to creep to the place where her husband had been slain. Sitting on the ground next to the cold body of her Moan-ee-yas (White Man), she kept a death vigil until dawn.

Ay-Ko-Skun knew that the miner would not hesitate to kill her and her young son or leave them with no horses or supplies to die of starvation in the wilderness. Her mind was clear. She knew what she had to do. By the first light of dawn, she whispered to her dead husband, "I will avenge you."

A short time later, she returned to the camp, started a small fire and made a breakfast of boiled meat and bannock. When the miner awoke, he came to her fire and asked her for the bag of food. Ay-Ko-Skun pointed toward a stump and served him his breakfast. Then she put her plan into action. While the murderer sat with his back to the smoking fire, she silently took the splitting axe from where it had been propped up against the roots of a pine. Summoning all her strength, she raised the heavy axe over her head and, with all the force she could muster, brought it down and smashed the miner's skull. He fell forward, thrashing for a moment or two until he lay still before the smouldering fire.

When Ay-Ko-Skun was sure that he was dead, she called to her son, and together they pulled Lemmon's body to the diggings on a blanket. Carefully, they placed the bags of gold on Lemmon's chest, keeping only a small handful of the gold, then covered the body with a pile of brush. Loading their food and supplies on a pack horse, they left the camp with Ay-Ko-Skun riding a second horse and her son riding his pinto pony. Silently, they headed high into the mountains in a westerly direction.

About a mile into the bush, Ay-Ko-Skun tethered the horses and, leaving her son to watch them, made her way back to the cabin. As she walked through the camp on her way to the diggings, she passed the cold campfire and the silent body of the murdered miner. When Ay-Ko-Skun reached the diggings, her heart was broken and bitter. Standing near the body of the man she had learned to love and respect, she vowed that he would have his gold in the Happy Hunting Ground. She then placed a curse on the diggings, so that no white man could take the gold that belonged to her Moan-ee-yas. The curse would drive men insane or cause them to die a horrible death in the wilderness. Only when her husband's spirit was at peace and his bones had crumbled to dust would a man with First Nations blood find the gold.

Ay-Ko-Skun's plan was simple. She placed some of the miners' blasting powder under a rock ledge over the diggings. When this was done, she lit the fuse and ran as quickly as she could into the bush. Several minutes later, she felt the earth heave and roll as a rockslide swept over the diggings and the camp, burying Lemmon and his gold.

That night, Ay-Ko-Skun and her son made a cold camp. The following day, the clouds opened and it began to rain, continuing for days. The trail was wild and the bush tangled. Many times, Ay-Ko-Skun had to stop to cut a path through the dense thickets. Travelling through strange country, she lost her bearings.

Ay-Ko-Skun and her son were now trying to head toward the south. They came to a river and had to swim their horses across the swollen stream. On another day, a grizzly bear caused the pack horse to break his lead rope and gallop, panic-stricken, back along the trail. After calming the remaining horses, they travelled only a short distance before making a small camp. They then spent several days in a futile search for the missing pack horse. Perhaps in its panic it had lost its footing on the slippery rocks and plunged over a cliff into the dark forest below. Regardless of what had happened, they had lost all their supplies.

The only piece of gear remaining after this disaster was Ay-Ko-Skun's rifle. Unfortunately, most of the bullets had been on the missing pack horse, and Ay-Ko-Skun was down to only five. They continued on in the rain, cold, starving and miserable, and came to a raging river. The stream was in full flood, carrying trees and clumps of bush in its boiling current. Unable to cross, Ay-Ko-Skun and her son made camp just about where the town of Sparwood is today.

Just when everything seemed bleak, their luck began to change. Ay-Ko-Skun managed to kill a small deer, and the little carcass provided some nourishment for the pair. After three days, the rain stopped, and Ay-Ko-Skun knew they must attempt a crossing of the river. To stay would surely mean starvation.

Tying her son's feet under the belly of his pony with a piece of rope, Ay-Ko-Skun mounted her horse and made herself ready. The frightened horses hesitated at the water's edge before being lashed into the foaming water. With her son yelling a war whoop, Ay-Ko-Skun answered with a Blood war chant as they were swept along in the powerful current. They were carried some distance downstream before their exhausted horses were able to struggle up the muddy bank on the opposite shore.

Wet and tired, they made camp there for the night. The following day they made their way across the mountains and over the summit of the Crowsnest Pass, eventually reaching the place where the town of Coleman, Alberta, is today. They made camp there and spent the night in a small teepee in the trees.

The next day, Ay-Ko-Skun and her son reached the home of Florence Kroesing's mother, who was living where the Charlie Sartoris sawmill is presently located in Coleman. Although taken in and doctored by Florence's mother, it was some time before the pair were well enough to travel on to their reserve at Cardston.

Three years later, Ay-Ko-Skun and her son returned to Coleman to thank Florence's mother for saving their lives. Ay-Ko-Skun brought gifts of beaded goods and asked Florence's mother to accompany her to the diggings. She wished to retrieve an HBC axe that Lemmon had given her.

The following morning, a small party consisting of Ay-Ko-Skun, several Bloods from the reserve, Florence, her mother and her little sister set out. That night, they made camp near a small island in the Livingstone River. The next morning, Florence and her little sister were left in the care of a woman from the reserve, while her mother, Ay-Ko-Skun and five braves went on to the diggings.

Florence concludes, "When we awoke the next morning, they were all back, without the axe. Everything had been covered with an avalanche, except a few stumps where the woman used to chop down trees. I only know part of the way. As far as I know, my mother was the only outsider who knew the way to the Lemmon Mine, which is still much sought-after with its treasure of gold."

It is quite easy to assign an approximate year to this account of the Lost Lemon Mine, because it is a matter of record that Florence Kroesing was born in 1895. As Florence claimed to have remembered the trip, it seems unlikely that she would have been younger than three or four years old. This indicates that the trip took place around the turn of the century, or perhaps the late 1890s at the earliest. This date is significantly later than the first newspaper accounts, but the tale of Ay-Ko-Skun remains a fascinating addition to the lore of the Lost Lemon Mine.

2

The Desperado Stories

THE GOLDFIELDS OF THE 1860S were a rough and ready place. Men were quick to take offence, and matters were usually settled with fists or pistols. Fisherville, situated on Wild Horse Creek in British Columbia, was one of the wildest gold camps in western Canada during the gold rush of the 1860s. Although little more than a shack town of about 50 buildings, Fisherville boasted saloons, dance halls, whorehouses and a brewery—in fact, places to indulge just about every vice one might care to mention. Shootouts and murders were common, and as always, the gold rush seemed to attract gamblers, bushwhackers and highwaymen, all eager to shake golden nuggets from the pockets of honest, hard-working miners.

One of the best descriptions of the desperadoes who preyed on the miners of Wild Horse Creek comes to us from John "Kootenai" Brown. A friend of Lafayette French, Brown recorded the stories of his adventures in the Cariboo goldfields and his days as a special constable at Wild Horse Creek:

> Three men came into Wild Horse and succeeded in passing several thousand dollars worth of bogus gold dust. It was an amalgam composed of 75% copper, 5% lead, and 20% gold. It was a very good imitation. The nuggets were made by dropping the molten metal from a high building. The fall made them exactly the shape of real nuggets.
>
> Well, these three fellows: Kirby, Conklin, and a third, whose name I forget, he was one of the desperadoes who helped to kill the Jews [this is a reference to three Jewish miners who were killed at Boston Bar for their gold dust, discussed in another part of Brown's account] and was afterwards hanged at Florence, these three brought in the amalgam, bought goods and paid for them with it. They were pointed out to me at once, and I marked them as suspicious-looking characters. When it was discovered that a lot of bogus nuggets were in circulation at the Creek I went to arrest the three strangers. They were living in a one-roomed cabin, and I knocked at the door. Getting no reply I burst open the door and Kirby grabbed for his gun. I had him covered and I called out to him, "Throw up your hands or I'll make a lead mine of your carcass."
>
> While I was getting Kirby out of the cabin the other two escaped. After putting my prisoner under lock and key I

organized a posse, and we were not long in locating Conklin and his pal, who were also put behind the bars. Just after this happened, and before the prisoners could be brought to trial, I got an appointment as a guard at the penitentiary at New Westminster, and left Wild Horse Creek. My successor, whom I recommended to Judge Cox as a suitable man for the job, had a streak of bad luck with the three men I left him in the jail.

Among the pieces of good advice I offered the young fellow was never to allow more than one prisoner out at one time, and never on any account to turn his back on a prisoner. I regret to say that one morning he thoughtlessly disregarded this advice and let all three out at one time to wash for breakfast. He turned his back for a moment, when Conklin "put the mug on him" (threw his arm under his chin and held his head back), then gagged and tied him.

Then they took his horse and what money he had, his clothes and his gun, and made a clean getaway. The jail was in a lonely part of the Creek and their escape was not known until the butcher called for the meat order. He knocked at the door but got no answer. He returned with a blacksmith, the lock was pried off and on entering they found the constable bound and gagged and locked in a cell, but the cells of the prisoners were empty. A search party was organized but no trace of the desperadoes was ever found.

About a week after the incident related above, the young constable, Hubble was his name, was shot. A murder was reported up the creek and Hubble went in search of the murderer. Hubble caught up with him about four miles out of Wild Horse Creek at a tributary called Brewery Creek. The fellow saw the constable pursuing him and jumped behind a tree. Hubble was green at the business and instead of ordering the villain out or getting help, he advanced singlehanded . . . The outlaw shot Hubble in the middle of the forehead. Then he grabbed the dead man's horse and dashed off down the trail. A bunch of miners happened along, saw what had occurred and pursued the murderer. After exchanging a few shots, a miner's bullet found a vital spot in his carcass and he rolled off the horse, dead.

Brown's account gives a vivid portrayal of the chaotic and violent gold-rush era and certainly illustrates the plausibility of the Lost Lemon Mine desperado stories that follow. These stories raise the very real possibility that the gold was not mined by Lemon and a partner, but stolen from prospectors.

The Neil Nicholson Papers

The first of the desperado stories concerning the Lost Lemon Mine comes from the Neil Nicholson collection, which is housed at the Glenbow Archives in Calgary. Born in Belfast, Prince Edward Island, in 1881, Nicholson joined the NWMP in 1900 and was given regimental number 3521. Normally, NWMP recruits had to be 21 years of age, but Nicholson managed to join up early.

In May 1900, Nicholson was sent to Fort Macleod, then later the same year he was transferred to the Porcupine Hills detachment. As he patrolled the area from Fort Macleod to the Crowsnest Pass, he heard stories about the Lost Lemon

Mine from old-timers. In 1905, after his term with the NWMP was up, Nicholson turned to cattle ranching. He later served with distinction during the First World War and was awarded the Military Medal for bravery in the field at Vimy Ridge.

After the war, Nicholson returned to ranching, remaining in the Porcupine Hills until moving to Cowley, Alberta, in 1947, and Calgary in 1952. Nicholson remained a bachelor until the age of 92, when he married Winnifred. He passed away at the Bow View Nursing Home on July 22, 1981, at the age of 100.

Nicholson wrote the following account for the Glenbow Archives in November 1961. Although he makes no mention of the year in which the incidents he relates occurred, it is likely that they took place between 1864, when gold was discovered in Wild Horse Creek, and 1873, when the NWMP established their barracks at Fort Macleod. While this fascinating account is by no means as well known as Dan Riley's, it may hold some clues to the location of the Lost Lemon Mine.

> For the past more than sixty years I have been hearing and reading stories about the Lost Lemon Mine.
>
> The original story put the location of the mine in the Kootenay district of British Columbia, but the later ones say that the mine was located in the mountains and the head of the Highwood River. Whether or not the mine ever existed will likely never be proved, but there is one thing of which

we may be 99 percent sure, and that is, it was not located in the Highwood area.

Many geological surveys of these mountains have been made, particularly since the discovery of oil in Alberta, and the geologists tell us that there is no gold in the east slopes of the Rockies, in the area between the Highwood and the Crowsnest Pass. In addition to this, the country has been prospected for the past nearly one hundred years and although I have lived in and covered much of the area involved, I have never heard of the slightest trace of gold ever having been found in this territory.

In June of 1900, I was sent out to the Porcupine Detachment of the N.W.M.P. located on Beaver Creek at the south end of the Porcupine Hills, thirty miles west of Fort Macleod. My district which I patrolled regularly extended from Fort Macleod westward to the Crowsnest Pass and north of the Old Man River to the Willow Creek watershed. This country took in what might be called the Lemon Mine area, and the story of the mine was well known to all the Old Timers living on what is known as the North Fork.

At that time, amongst the many pioneers who lived in the North Fork district, were four men, who were part of a group of buffalo hunters. They came to that part of Alberta in the late sixties and when the buffalo were all killed off they settled on land in the North Fork district.

When on patrol I called on some of these men regularly and talked with them on many occasions about the early days. They had an entirely different story to tell about the Lost Lemon Mine.

These four men, whose names were: William Olin,

John Nelson, Mort [Matt] Holloway, and William Lee, were in that country at the time Lemon had made the gold strike.

They claimed that the strike was made in the Kootenay country of British Columbia and that Lemon, after killing Black Jack, was making his escape to Fort Benton, through the Dutch Creek Pass, and buried the gold somewhere on the North Fork.

Sam Livingston, another pioneer, was in this part of the country at this time. He moved to the north about 1875 where he settled on the Elbow River near where Calgary now stands. He also said the gold was found in the Kootenay Country and perhaps high-jacked by Lemon and his partner.

I will tell the story of Lemon's Mine as those pioneer buffalo hunters of the North Fork country told it to me in the early years of the century.

Lemon and Black Jack were prospectors who worked out of Spokane. In those days Spokane was a lively camp and quite a centre with prospectors working out in all directions. An old friend of mine, Clarence Hughston, who had lived in Spokane during these years and who later settled west of Granum, often told me yarns of the prospectors in Spokane, or Spokane Falls, as he always referred to it.

From Spokane, Lemon and Black Jack prospected north into Canada. They would hit the Kootenay River about where Bonners Ferry now stands and work up on the east side, panning for gold as they went.

As future events have proven, the first gold that they would strike would be in the Fort Steele area.

In later years, much gold was taken out of the Wild Horse district.

They may have made their strike there. In any event,

when winter was setting in they returned to Spokane with a poke of gold. In the spring, with a new grub stake, they returned to their digging. From this point there are two different stories. One to the effect that Lemon and Black Jack high-jacked the gold and were making their escape to Fort Benton; the other, that they worked their claim and accumulated a large quantity of gold.

Lemon now decided to kill Black Jack and take all the gold himself, but when he did this, he could not return to Spokane without having a lot of explaining to do about what had happened to his partner. So he decided to go to Fort Benton. He knew the Forts on the Old Man River, Fort Kipp, Fort Whoop-up, and if he could get to the Old Man River near its headwaters he would have no difficulty in getting to Fort Benton.

Here is where Chief Bear Paw [*sic*] came into the picture.

It had been the custom for years for the Stoney Indians, particularly the band that lived on the Highwood, to make an excursion each summer to the Kootenay country to engage in horse races, sports and gambling with the Kootenai Indians. They continued this practice up to my time, as in 1902 I was called upon by a rancher to follow them and recover a stolen horse. They told me they were just returning from their usual visit with the Kootenais.

The route followed by these Indians would be along what is now the Coleman Kananaskis highway. They would follow the Livingstone and the Old Man Rivers till they came to Dutch Creek, named after Dutch Frank, a prospector and trapper who lived there in the early days. They would go up Dutch Creek, through the Dutch Creek Pass, striking the Elk River a few miles north of Natal. They would follow the

Elk till they hit the Kootenay, then up that river to the Fort Steele area, where the Kootenay Indians made their headquarters.

Lemon, after killing Black Jack, made a deal with Chief Bearspaw to guide him through the mountains to the Old Man River, which the story says he did. From that point, Bearspaw went north to his camping grounds and Lemon went south on his own. Here is where the mystery begins. My memory of this part of the story is somewhat vague, but the general impression was that Lemon was being chased, and to make his escape, he buried the gold somewhere between Dutch Creek and the Gap; or even below the Gap. Who was chasing Lemon is not clear. Perhaps this is where the high jacking story could fit in.

There must have been very sound grounds for the assumption that he buried his gold in this area, because in later years, even up to the nineties, each summer John Nelson and Mort [Matt] Holloway would saddle up their ponies, and with a pack outfit, they would go through the Gap, looking not for the Lemon Mine, but rather in search of the spot where Lemon hid his gold. It does not seem logical that these pioneers would do this year after year if they did not have some very good grounds to think that the gold was there.

Even myself, when I was road foreman putting a new road in through the Gap, forty years ago, I had in the back of my mind the thought that we might run our grader into the Lemon gold cache.

Signed, N. Nicholson

Fred Kennedy's Account

The second of the desperado stories comes to us from veteran newspaperman Fred Kennedy of Calgary. Born in Dundee, Scotland, Kennedy first came to Calgary in 1912, where he worked as a sportswriter, political writer, city editor, police reporter and columnist for over 55 years. Kennedy died in 1988.

In 1931, as a reporter for the *Calgary Daily Herald*, Kennedy covered a mini–gold rush that occurred in the Livingstone Range. At that time, he came in contact with King Bearspaw and some of the Stoneys at Morley. He also spoke with John Hunter (Chief Sitting Eagle) of the Stoneys, who told him a version of the Lost Lemon Mine story known to his people. Kennedy wrote about this in his book *Alberta Was My Beat*, and the following is based upon that account.

In the winter of 1870, a hunting party of Stoneys led by Chief Jacob Bearspaw made a trip into the Rockies in search of game. It had been a hard winter with much snow, and the supplies of the tribe were running low. Saddling their ponies, the Stoneys rode out of the settlement at Morley and headed south into the Livingstone Range. Sometime during this trip, they came upon the camp of two white men. One man sat half-starved and near-demented in front of a small campfire, while his partner lay dead and frozen in the snow. Two worn-out saddle horses were tethered nearby. When questioned by Chief Bearspaw, the survivor said his name was Jack Lemon, or Blackjack, as he was known by other prospectors. He then related a confused story about the events that had led to the death of his partner.

According to Lemon, he and his partner, known as Dancing Bill, had made a strike somewhere in the vicinity, but when they had tried to bring out the gold, they had been ambushed on the trail. Lemon said they had managed to escape their attackers, but his partner had been shot in the back and died shortly thereafter of his wounds.

The Stoneys remained in Lemon's camp for two days. During that time, a quantity of gold dust and small nuggets were traded for tea, sugar and moose meat. Lemon also traded his worn-out horses for two of the Stoneys' ponies. Lemon told the Stoneys of his "mine" in the mountains and how he planned to return sometime the following spring to recover the rest of the gold. He admitted that he was lost and stated that he and his partner were trying to return to the United States when they had been ambushed. The Stoneys provided him with a rough map that showed him how to reach a pass that would lead him into the country around Lundbreck and Pincher Creek, then south across the border into Montana.

Several weeks later, while returning to Morley, the Stoneys met a group of American prospectors. The Stoneys traded a small amount of Lemon's gold for supplies and told the Americans about Lemon and his murdered partner. It seemed to the Stoneys that the two men might have had something to hide. Why would they have risked death and starvation crossing the high mountain passes in the dead of winter if they had not been running away from something or someone? Lemon had claimed to have found a mine, yet there was no ore in his pack. Instead, he had traded placer gold washed from river gravels. If the story of the gold was false, what then of the ambush and the murdered prospector? It seemed more likely that Lemon's gold came from the East Kootenay goldfields, which were very rich in placer gold. Maybe Lemon and his partner had panned their gold there. Of course, there was another explanation for Lemon's strange behaviour. Perhaps the two prospectors had committed murder and robbery in the East Kootenays, then Lemon had gunned down Dancing Bill to avoid splitting the gold after their escape over the Great Divide.

Chief Bearspaw seemed certain that Lemon and his partner had entered the Rockies from BC. When his camp was discovered by the Stoneys, Lemon had no idea where he was. If Lemon had entered the mountains from the east, he would certainly have marked his trail for the return trip. Given the fact that Bearspaw knew of no creeks east of the Great Divide that contained gold nuggets, it seemed only reasonable to conclude that Lemon had obtained his gold in BC, possibly by panning or more likely by murder.

According to Kennedy, there were many other versions of the Lost Lemon Mine story in circulation in the Pincher Creek area during the 1930s. Most of them seemed to suggest that Lemon hijacked the gold from the British Columbia goldfields, then shot his partner in the back.

Kennedy certainly reached his own conclusions with regard to Chief Sitting Eagle's account of the Lost Lemon Mine:

> I am also convinced that this gold was stolen from B.C. miners and that Lemon and Dancing Bill were fleeing from a miners' posse when they took to the mountains in an effort to cross the Great Divide and reach the safety of their home state of Montana. Only desperate and guilty men would have chosen such a dangerous route . . . As it was, "Dancing Bill" died with a bullet in his back and it was suggested that "Blackjack" had murdered his partner so that he could gain possession of all of the stolen gold.

Jimmy White's Account

The third and last of the desperado stories concerning the Lost Lemon Mine comes to us from Jimmy White, an old prospector who lived in the East Kootenay region at Fort Steele. What makes this account unique is that Jimmy White was the only person to speak about the Lost Lemon Mine from first-hand experience. He claimed to have met the mysterious Lemon in Fort Steele in the mid-1880s.

White's life is as mysterious as the lives of Lemon and Blackjack. Perhaps that's not surprising, since both White and Lemon were miners and prospectors, not given to volunteering many details about their personal lives or travels. What little information we have about White comes from Art and Bob Cantin, a father and son from Calgary who spent many years researching the mystery of the Lost Lemon Mine. They interviewed Jimmy White at Fort Steele in 1966 and recorded an audiotape on April 19, 1969, shortly before White's death. White gave his birthday as St. Patrick's Day, March 17, and stated that he first came to the goldfields in about 1885, when he was 12 years old. This would mean he was born in 1873, which supports White's statement to Bob Cantin that he was 93 during the summer of 1966.

White claimed to have been married to Klondike Kate sometime during the Klondike gold rush in the late 1890s. During this period, until just before the outbreak of the First World War, White spent time in the Klondike and on the west coast, either in Vancouver or Victoria. During his 1966 interview, White spoke of his years in the Klondike: "Gold was no good to anybody in that country . . . You had three things to do with it. You could spend it at the bootlegger, spend it at the gamblers, or you could give it to the garters."

There is a little information available on White in the archives at Fort Steele. However, it seems likely that Jimmy White was not, in fact, his legal name. His file states that he came to the Fort Steele area just prior to the outbreak of the First World War. It appears that he may have added 10 years to his actual age to avoid being drafted into the army and to avoid being accused of cowardice. He maintained this fiction with all but his closest friends until the time of his death. In the 1969 audiotape, White is heard telling several unidentified tourists that his age is 103.

From what Bob Cantin recalls of their conversations, White worked as a guide in the Fort Steele area when he was not prospecting, and he claimed to have acted as guide to "German chancellor" Paul Von Hindenburg (who wasn't actually chancellor but would become the second president of Germany), when he visited British Columbia some time before the outbreak of the First World War. White continued to mine in the Fort Steele area throughout his life and was still working several claims in 1966.

Information obtained from the 1969 audiotape states that White died on July 10, 1969. He was cremated, and his ashes were scattered near Canal Flats and on Wild Horse Creek. No other details are available on the life of White. The following account is based on notes from the 1966 interview.

White claimed to have first gone to the goldfields at Fort Steele when he was 12 or 13, around 1885. There he met Lemon, or Bill Lemon, as White called him. White described Lemon as a stocky character, about 5 feet 9 or 10 inches tall. Lemon was an unfriendly character, given to solitary drinking, or "buying Dick Smiths," as White and the old miners called it. Lemon seems to have been around town from time to time, for Jimmy remembered seeing him three or four times during his years at Fort Steele.

White remembered that Lemon once came into Fort Steele with a bullet wound in his leg and had reported it to the NWMP. This would have occurred in 1887 or 1888, as those were the only years that the NWMP maintained a detachment at Fort Steele. Lemon told the NWMP that Indians had shot his partner, Blackjack, which White recalled as being the nickname of a man named McGowan. Lemon was patched up, and when he was able to walk and ride, he left the area and returned to Montana.

It seems, however, that Blackjack was not dead. He thought he had killed Lemon and had hightailed it back to the United States. He ended up in a pesthouse (a sanatorium) in San Francisco, likely suffering from smallpox, and was cared for by a man called McIver. During his stay in San Francisco, Blackjack showed McIver a map that he had drawn. With the map as his guide, McIver journeyed north to the Fort Steele area. McIver was working on Finlay Creek when White first met him and saw the map supposedly drawn by Blackjack. White recalled that it was written on an old, very soft paper bag that had been rolled up. Bill Essay, a surveyor friend of White, helped McIver pinpoint the location indicated on the map

What follows is not recorded in Bob Cantin's original notes but is based on his recollection of the conversation with Jimmy White in 1966. I've been lucky to have a 25-year friendship with Bob and have spent many hours listening to his accounts of his days in the Fort Steele country, searching for the Lost Lemon Mine. Bob was a personal friend of Jimmy White and was one of the few people to whom Jimmy told his story. According to White, McIver's map showed the location of the cabin used by Blackjack and Lemon. Blackjack had told McIver there was gold buried in a hole in the floor of the shack. White was very adamant in stating that there never was a mine. According to him, Lemon and Blackjack were just bandits and bushwhackers and had stolen the gold from miners on the trail. White said that the foundation logs of Lemon's cabin were still there but that the area was overgrown, and it would be difficult to find. White did not know if any gold was still buried there, but he figured not. If there had been, it had been dug up long ago. White did not think much of Lemon, whom he called an "asshole" and a "bullshit artist."

In his interview notes, Bob Cantin recorded that when White last saw him, Bill Lemon was leading a party of five and heading into the Bull River country, south of Fort Steele. White remembered that Lemon's travelling companions became suspicious and seemed to think that Lemon was "jacking them around." (Although it is not stated in the interview notes, presumably Lemon had promised to lead the men to promising gold claims.) It seemed their patience was wearing thin and that if Lemon didn't produce, they would turn him over to the Mounties, either because they thought he had killed Blackjack or because they were convinced he had attempted to defraud them by leading them astray. Lemon left the area that night and was never seen in those parts again.

In 1966, Jimmy drew a copy of the map Blackjack had

given to McIver. This map survives in Bob Cantin's files, but while it shows that Lemon's cabin was located about one-half mile from a river up a feeder creek, Jimmy does not specify which river. Bob Cantin said that White did not want to start a rush, so he intentionally left out some important details on his map. "If Jimmy's map got printed in a book," said Cantin, "treasure hunters would be tramping around the bush, and it would make life mighty difficult for any folks working legitimate claims in the area. Besides, old Jimmy was sure that Lemon's gold had been dug up years ago, so he didn't know what all the fuss was about, anyway." However, Bob Cantin remembers that White said Lemon's cabin was within 15 miles of Fort Steele. The area had been burnt over when a forest fire passed through the region. The cabin was destroyed, but according to White, the foundation logs were still there in 1966.

Perhaps White did not want to spoil the mystery and wanted folks to figure out the hiding place of Lemon's gold for themselves. White had seen the gold rush to Wild Horse Creek and the stampede to the Klondike. He had seen men die from the cold and the heartache, and the one thing White knew about gold was that finding it was never easy.

3

The First Nations Stories

SEVERAL FIRST NATIONS STORIES SPEAK of lost gold, but it is possible that some of them may not be connected with the Lost Lemon Mine. While the evidence linking these accounts to the mystery is circumstantial, they should be included in any discussion of the Lost Lemon Mine as they may provide valuable clues to the solution of this puzzle.

The Files of Arthur Cantin

Arthur (Art) J. Cantin was born in Lowell, Massachusetts. He first came to Alberta in the early years of the century. His lifelong passions included automotive sports and a love of the outdoors and western Canadian history, notably the legend of Lost Lemon Mine.

According to Bob, his son, Art was frequently gripped by fits of wanderlust and gold fever and was always ready to head off into the mountains to check out a new lead or one of his theories concerning Lemon's gold. No doubt Art loved a good story and derived much pleasure from the time he spent hiking up wilderness trails looking for Lemon's lost Eldorado. Art Cantin died of a heart attack on July 26, 1984, at the age of 73.

While some people believe that the Lost Lemon Mine is somewhere in the upper reaches of the Highwood River, Cantin's account suggests that the Lost Lemon Mine is actually farther north, near the headwaters of the Clearwater River. The story begins in January 1894. It had been a terrible fall with the snows coming deep and early, driving most game animals off their usual ranges. Although the federal authorities were supposed to supply treaty Indians with cattle to replace the buffalo, which had been virtually exterminated from North America by the mid-1880s, this did not always happen. As a result, the Indians of the reserve were frequently forced to exist on a subsistence diet. Apparently, the severe weather had caused many deaths, and by January, they were getting desperate.

Colin Thompson was a homesteader living near the Little Red Deer River, situated in what is now Red Lodge Provincial Park, about 70 miles north and west of Calgary, near the town of Bowden. Two Cree braves, leading a string of eight pack horses, came from the west and took refuge from the storm at Thompson's place. They were completely done in and suffering terribly from the severe cold. Like most pioneers would have done, Thompson promptly took them in. The Crees warmed themselves around Thompson's wood stove and shared a meal with him and a trapper named Henning, who was visiting the household. As a result of Thompson's kindness, we may now hold an important clue to the mystery surrounding the Lost Lemon Mine.

The Crees, grateful for the reprieve from the storm, were ready to converse with their newfound friends. Fortunately, Thompson had worked as a factor for the HBC and could speak Cree, for the braves told an amazing story. It had been a winter of starvation and death. Before the tribe, camped in a protected foothills valley, could lay in a winter supply of meat, heavy snows had driven the animals out of the vicinity. Due to the snow, the tribe had been unable to travel, and they were forced to subsist on rabbits and grouse. Soon even this food source became scarce, and death came to the snowbound encampment, carrying off a number of babies and elders.

With their situation perilous, the chief called upon the two braves who now sat in Thompson's shanty. He instructed them to make the hazardous trip to the trading post at Bowden, on the eastern end of the valley, where they could obtain badly needed supplies. They had been travelling for eight days and were most grateful to Thompson for the food and shelter, for they were exhausted and might not have made the post at Bowden.

Thompson, having seen their horses, noted that they

had carried no furs or other trade goods. Curious, he asked the braves what they planned to barter at Bowden, since the post was not noted for its charity when it came to dealing with First Nations people. He inquired whether or not they planned to swap their horses for trade goods. The Crees answered in the negative, stating that all the horses would be needed to carry supplies back to their starving people.

When Thompson told the braves the storekeeper would give them nothing without something to trade, the older of the two Crees pulled out from his saddlebag two buckskin pokes packed with coarse gold and nuggets. He was certain the white trader at Bowden would have no objections to taking this instead.

The effect upon Thompson and Henning was immediate. Henning became wildly excited upon seeing the gold and wanted to know where it had come from. The Crees answered that the gold had come from a sacred valley. However, when pressed for more details, they would just say that the location was taboo and was known only to the chief and medicine man. The gold was to be used in extreme emergencies, such as the one in which the tribe now found itself. The chief had given the braves just enough gold to pay for the white man's supplies.

Henning was convinced that there must be much more gold at the diggings and questioned the Crees about the location of the find. As Henning's questions became more probing, the two men became reluctant to discuss the matter further, but they did say that the gold was near a First Nations burial ground.

Henning offered them his pack outfit, his horses, rifle, traps and pelts—in fact, everything he owned—if the Crees would take him to the location of the secret valley. The Crees, no doubt seeing Henning's excitement and knowing of the white man's madness for the yellow metal, refused his offer and insisted that they must leave at once for the trading post. As they rode toward Bowden, 10 miles to the east, Henning made plans to follow them when they returned to the mountains and their tribe.

Perhaps the Crees suspected Henning's intentions, for they went home by another route. Henning waited at the homestead for several days before realizing that the Crees would not return, and before he could backtrack along their original trail, a snowstorm obliterated their tracks toward the mountains. Henning estimated the Crees had travelled about 100 miles before they reached the Thompson homestead. In later years, Colin Thompson again met the two Cree braves, who told him that the gold had indeed saved the tribe that terrible winter.

In an article that appeared in *Golden West* magazine in 1968, Bob Cantin stated that the sacred valley of which the Cree spoke and the Lost Lemon Mine could have been the same place:

The Old Rocky Mountain House trading post was situated on the North Saskatchewan River, a well-known gold-bearing stream on the eastern side of the Rockies. To the south and west of Rocky Mountain House are other gold-bearing streams, all flowing easterly. But to the south and west of Morley, there are no gold-bearing streams east of the continental divide. The old Indian trail which leads south from Rocky Mountain House traverses both these areas. Is it not reasonable to assume that Blackjack and Lemon could have followed one of these more northerly streams to the Mother Lode, the sacred spot of the Crees, and perhaps the Stoney Indians.

Now, Blackjack and Lemon were Americans, working out of Fort Benton or the Tobacco Plains. Normally, they would have headed home by the shortest route. The shortest road home was in a southerly direction, whether they started from Mist Mountain, High River, or Rocky Mountain House. To get to Fort Benton from High River or the area near Mist Mountain, they would have travelled south-easterly to Fort Macleod, Fort Kipp, and Fort Hamilton (Fort Whoop-up), then south on the wagon road to Fort Benton.

Being about 75 miles or more south of Morleyville, it is unlikely that Chief Bearspaw could always be aware of their presence in that area.

But on the other hand, if they came from west of Bowden and travelled south to either Fort Benton or to the Tobacco Plains, their route was straight through Bearspaw's territory, as the Indian trail from Rocky Mountain House passed directly through Morleyville.

Can we not further assume that the mine could be somewhere near this northernmost trail? Possibly 100 miles west of Bowden, which figured in the starving Indian episode? There is gold in the area south of Rocky Mountain House, none in the area south of Morley.

This may explain why the Lost Lemon Mine has not been found south of Morley on the Highwood River, even though people have been scouring the area for over 100 years.

Cantin's article concludes by adding an even more dramatic clue to the possible solution of the Lost Lemon Mine mystery. While the story of Colin Thompson, the starving Crees and their gold dust is central to Cantin's theory, he ends his article with a revelation that may prove that he was on the right track in determining the location of Lemon's lost mine:

At the present time, this writer, with the information and guidance of a friend and hunting companion, recently found a valley in the mountains west of Bowden that has all the known requirements of the Lost Lemon Mine. A once well-travelled trail, long abandoned and overgrown, the confluence of three-creeks, etc. It is somewhere west of Red Lodge Provincial Park at a distance of about eight days' ride. But most important of all, there is a hole that looks suspiciously like a mine entrance, nestled high on the side of a mountain that will remain at the moment nameless.

Fearing the wrath of Wah-con-dah, we dared not climb to investigate, the month being June, the weather warm, and another avalanche all set to be triggered by some clumsy paleface. We were content to examine this possible location with the spotting scope from the other side of the valley about half a mile away. It was visible from a narrow angle only. A man could glass the slope for days and not see the hole unless he was in just the right place and looked in the right direction. Big John, our mountain friend and hunter, on a thousand-to-one chance, spotted it when the bighorn sheep he was hunting passed near. It is a sure bet we will take a good look next summer when the slopes are dry and firm, making a climb to the spot for a first-hand inspection.

So, friends, make your own conclusions. North or south? The old Indian trail is now a Forestry service road, passable to Jeeps and other vehicles in the summer. The grandson of Chief Jacob Bearspaw, King Bearspaw, now in his seventies, has spent most of his life looking for the mine in this same valley.

This is certainly a fascinating tale. In my discussions with Bob Cantin, he told me of the occasion, some time in the late 1950s, when he and his father met up with King Bearspaw in this same valley. According to their discussions with the forest ranger who had been stationed in the region for about 15 years, they learned that King Bearspaw had been coming to prospect in this valley for as long as the ranger had been at his posting. It seems unlikely that Bearspaw, a man who had a direct connection with the story through his father, Chief Moses Bearspaw, would have spent so many years searching this valley for the location of the mine if it were, as the popular theory proposed, 100 miles to the south.

Unfortunately, Art Cantin never succeeded in entering the cave that may have held the secret of the Lost Lemon Mine. When they returned the following year, a slide had destroyed the trail leading up from the valley to the mouth of the tiny chamber. The cave was cut in a vertical face of sheer rock, and it was not possible to gain access to the chamber without climbing gear or a helicopter. Other circumstances prevented Art and Bob from investigating the cave in the following years, and it now seems that the exact location of the cave has been lost. Fortunately, Bob was able to locate a photograph of the mysterious cave that his father had taken that long-ago June.

Another interesting item from Art Cantin's personal archives is an audiotape on which Cantin recorded an old story from the fur-trading journals concerning gold. The story is also found in Kerry Wood's book *A Corner of Canada*. It was recorded in the journals that a Cree man who traded at Rocky Mountain House was known to have cast the bullets for his muzzle loader out of pure gold. Unfortunately, there is no mention in the account as to the possible source of this gold.

Another story from this audiotape concerns stolen gold at Red Deer. Is this another clue to the existence of a lost mine west of Bowden?

A Mrs. Bella Johnson who did housework around Red Deer around 1910 to 25 was an Indian woman who confided to her white friends that this same gold had killed her husband. He supposedly found the cache and brought out over $1,000 worth of dust. Shortly afterward he died and his wife was firmly convinced that his death was due to a violation of the tribal taboo. This area is due west of Bowden and places it in the same general area as the Red Deer ranger station around which King Bearspaw was searching through a great many summers of his life.

In 1968, Art Cantin photographed a vertical rock face with a cave that he believed might have held clues to the secret of the Lost Lemon Mine. BOB CANTIN

The source of this story is uncertain, and no other details are known concerning these anecdotes. If they are true, they certainly add weight to Cantin's theory that the Lost Lemon Mine is located somewhere along the Clearwater River west of Bowden, toward Rocky Mountain House.

A Variation of Colin Thompson's Story
Colin Thompson, the man who had taken the Cree braves

in from the cold, was born in the village of Rosemarkie, Scotland, on September 3, 1855. He joined the HBC in 1875 and served in several HBC posts over the years: The Pas, Grand Rapids, Fort Stanley and Norway House. During his service at The Pas, he met Sarah Margaret Macdonald, whom he married on July 28, 1884, in Winnipeg.

In 1892, Thompson left the employ of the HBC and returned to Scotland with his family. They came back to Canada in 1895 and settled in the Red Lodge area, 10 miles west of the present town of Bowden, along the Little Red Deer River. Thompson operated a trading post at Red Lodge for several years and served as postmaster until the time of his death on February 4, 1931.

Another tale concerning Thompson and the Cree braves who were carrying gold dust is entitled "Red Gold" and comes from the files of the Bowden Historical Society. The account is at odds with that recorded by Art Cantin, and it is not possible to say with any certainty which version is correct. It seems likely that this tale, like many others connected with the Lost Lemon Mine, has undergone subtle changes with each telling. What follows is based on this account.

One day while Thompson was trading or selling some goods to several trapper-prospectors, two Cree braves who were unknown to Thompson entered the trading post. They selected a number of food items but had no money to pay for the purchase, offering instead a quantity of red gold, which is placer gold that contains traces of copper. As you can imagine, this red gold caused a great deal of excitement among the prospectors who were dealing with Thompson, and they began to question the Crees as to the source of the gold. The Crees' replies were noncommittal, but this only seemed to increase the prospectors' interest. The prospectors became more and more inquisitive, until the Crees, weary of the questions, beat a retreat and hurried out of the trading post. A few moments later, the prospectors gathered up their gear and also left the post, presumably in search of the braves. It is thought that the prospectors caught up with the Crees and tried to force the secret location of the red gold from them. According to the story, neither the white men nor the Crees were seen again. This led to speculation that the Crees may have murdered the white prospectors to keep the secret of the red gold, or perhaps the braves were murdered after confessing their secrets to the prospectors; however, it is not possible to state with any certainty what happened to any of them.

The account does say that red gold was very uncommon in the Bowden area, and that very little red gold had been seen since the Crees visited Thompson's post at Red Lodge. Did the red gold come from Lemon's diggings?

The Chronicle of King Bearspaw

King Bearspaw, who died in April 1979 at the age of 89, was the final living link to the mystery of the Lost Lemon

Mine. The son of Chief Moses Bearspaw, King Bearspaw devoted more than 70 years of his life to searching for the fabled mine.

King Bearspaw's grandfather, Chief Jacob Bearspaw, first learned about Blackjack's murder from the two Stoney braves who had witnessed it. The names of these braves in Dan Riley's version of the story are given as William and Daniel Bendow. In the 1950s, Dr. Hugh Dempsey, an archivist with the Glenbow Institute, concluded that the surname Bendow was unknown among the three Stoney bands: the Wesley, Chiniki and Bearspaw. Indeed, a search of the treaty list for 1877 shows no trace of the name. As Riley's version of the story has William Bendow present at Blackjack's murder and meeting with Lafayette French in 1912, the year of his death, this apparent contradiction must be addressed.

While the name Bendow never appears on the treaty lists, the names Daniel and Paul Bigman do appear in 1917. It is interesting to note that Daniel Bigman was 16 years old in 1870, the year of Blackjack's murder, and that one of the children listed under Paul Bigman's ticket (the listing of affiliated members of his family on the reserve) was a young boy by the name of King Bearspaw. Although no mention of the Bendows appears anywhere, "Bigman" is the only similar surname that appears, and the fact that King Bearspaw was part of the family affiliated with Bigman suggests there may have been a connection.

King Bearspaw began his search for the Lost Lemon Mine in 1907. An article by Tom Primrose in the *Nanton News* of July 24, 1959, quotes King Bearspaw speaking about his early interest in the mysterious mine: "I've had it in my blood since I was a boy. It's been a dream to me all my life and I guess I'd sooner look for the Lost Lemon Mine than do anything else. My grandmother said it was alright to look for it. My mother told me not to look for the mine because if I found it the gold would bring unhappiness and maybe death. I've kept on looking all these years. I don't think the gold would have done me any harm, if I'd found it."

When asked whether he believed that the Lost Lemon Mine existed, Bearspaw replied:

"Oh yes, it's there, somewhere. My grandfather knew where it was, but he would never tell anyone where. He told me all about it, except where the mine was. He and his two brothers knew. One of the brothers saw the murder committed over the gold Lemon and Blackjack found. None of them would tell where the gold is."

King Bearspaw went on to say that none of the young people were interested in hearing about these things now. He was of the opinion that the old chief did not keep the location of the mine secret because of his dislike of gold or white men, but because the finding of gold would have brought in a rush of gold seekers, and the good hunting grounds would have been destroyed. King Bearspaw concluded by saying, "He had no use for the gold, I have."

The secret of the Lost Lemon Mine's location passed from Chief Jacob Bearspaw to King's father, Chief Moses Bearspaw. However, because of King's professed interest in finding the mine and his desire to use the gold, the secret was never passed on to him and died with Chief Moses Bearspaw. In 1921, King Bearspaw gave up his rights as a treaty Indian to be free to travel the backcountry off the reserve, looking for the lost mine.

On February 16, 1931, an article in the *Calgary Daily Herald* reported on an ill-fated gold rush at the head of Livingstone Creek:

In 1931, rumors of gold brought hordes of eager fortune hunters to the foot of Mount Sentinel Pass west of High River.

Poorly equipped, few got further than the bottom of the eastern side of the pass. Those who did struggle on to the Livingstone found nothing but worthless fool's gold or iron pyrites.

Fred Kennedy, reporter for the *Calgary Herald*, ventured into the mountains on horseback to either prove or disprove the gold rush. Kennedy and his group headed out from the Buffalo Head ranch on the Highwood River.

The first night out they had the good fortune to come across the camp of King Bearspaw, who was returning from a hunting trip. After some discussion, Bearspaw agreed to accompany Kennedy and his group over the Pass. About two hours after they left, a sudden blizzard struck. Bearspaw urged them on, saying it was now or never. During the storm, one of their pack horses was caught by the wind and overturned, falling from the trail to break its back when it landed in the crotch of a tree.

Finally reaching Livingstone Creek, they had hoped to wash samples of ore for gold, but were prevented as the creek bed was bone dry. They met up with Senator Dan Riley and his three sons, who had arrived on the Livingstone before them. No gold was found and the samples collected failed to impress either Riley or Kennedy. On their way out, they were met by dozens of gold seekers heading into the region, and managed to convince most of those they met that it was a fool's mission.

Finally with Kennedy's help, the RCMP managed to convince the public that the gold rush was a hoax, and before long, the whole thing fizzled out.

This was one version of events, but there was another. George Pocaterra, the retired rancher and prospector who led the expedition for the *Calgary Daily Herald* in 1931, talked about this trip in an article published by the newspaper on November 9, 1961. In this article, he also said he was very skeptical about the Lost Lemon Mine and doubted whether it ever existed. It was Pocaterra's opinion that Lemon and Blackjack probably stole the gold dust from miners in the Kootenay Mountains of BC, then hiked out over the mountains into the High River country. "Lemon probably murdered his partner to avoid splitting the robbery loot, then made up the story about the mine to cover his deeds." Pocaterra concluded by saying, "That's the story that makes sense to me."

Pocaterra's version of the events that transpired on the 1931 trip is at odds with some of the other accounts published in the media. In a letter Pocaterra wrote to the editor of *The Albertan*, which was published on November 11, 1961, he attempts to set the record straight:

In February, 1931 I had a phone call from *The Herald* telling me about the gold rush then taking place to the head of the Livingstone River, and asking me if I were willing to take charge and guide a party to investigate the supposed strike, and also to provide all the necessary riding and pack horses and camp equipment for the trip, and when I agreed to do so I was told that they would send a reporter to write up the story, and then put me in touch with Fred Kennedy, to who I gave a list of needed provisions I wanted him to bring up to my Buffalo Head Ranch from Calgary. He drove up to the ranch, from where, next day, we rode to the head of the Livingstone River, over the Sentinel Mountain Pass, where the gold strike was supposed to have taken place, arriving at dusk. It was an unbelievably fine day for that time of the year, a strong and very warm chinook wind blowing, and certainly no sign of a blizzard as stated in the story, and no horse fell and broke its back, and I wonder what made Kennedy dream up that story about the blizzard and the horse with the broken back!

As King Bearspaw had been camping near my ranch, I had hired him to come along to help with the packing and making camp. We found several hundred people making up the rush, and quite a number were camped at the head of the Livingstone. King and I made camp and as soon as possible put up the tin stove and started melting snow for tea, as the river was dry there. Next morning King and I climbed a short way, no more than a quarter of a mile, to the location of the supposed gold-bearing stream, and I broke off twenty pounds of samples with my prospector's hammer. Those samples were the ones that *The Herald*, later on, had analyzed and found to be worthless. The Mounted Police then got all the people out, and lucky it was that the weather stayed warm. Had there been a real blizzard, many of the people would not have been able to make it back to civilization.

Yours truly, George W. Pocaterra

This fascinating letter shows that newspaper reports may sometimes be at odds with the facts, although there may now be no way of knowing which version of the story is correct.

Also meriting closer scrutiny is King Bearspaw's role in the discovery of the gold sample that sparked the rush in the first place. On February 16, 1931, the *Calgary Daily Herald* printed the following item:

On October 16, 1930, King Bearspaw of the Stoneys found a piece of quartz near the summit of Flat Mountain, a peak about 5000 feet high that rises out of the east side of the Livingstone Valley. It looked like rich ore. He told Jack Hagerman, of High River, of his find. The three men went back in and claims were staked.

Whether or not the piece of quartz contained gold is not yet known, but the strange thing about it is that no other ore of a similar kind has been found in the vicinity of the original find, and this has given rise to the belief that the quartz found by Bearspaw had "floated" down from somewhere.

However, an intriguing letter to the editor of the *Calgary Daily Herald*, published on March 6, 1931, seems to throw a different light on this matter and may help to clear up the mystery.

Editor, *The Herald*: I have just been reading in the *Daily Herald* of Feb. 16 the account of the gold boom on the Livingstone River west of Nanton. As I have lived for over twenty years about 25 miles southwest of High River, and hunted and prospected the country around Sentinel Mountain and the Livingstone River so much, maybe I can throw a little light on a subject that seems to be puzzling so many, namely the source of the mineral that King Bearspaw found . . . In the summer of 1920 I was at Trail, B.C. and while visiting the smelter I picked up a pocket of what looked to me to be gold bearing quartz. I don't want you to think I stole it, as that wasn't what I called it at all. I picked this stuff from where it had been dropped, either in unloading cars or in transferring it to the smelter, and there was lots of it lying around, the same as there is coal laying around a coal yard.

Now this stuff that was undoubtedly rich lay around our house till one day in 1923, a few days after the big flood, when King Bearspaw stopped at the house, and the conversation turned to gold, I showed him what we had, and gave some of it to him. There is an old saying that if you keep a thing seven years you will find a use for it, and it looks to me as if King had found a use for that little bit of stuff I gave him seven years ago.

With a gold boom on, pack ponies and guides will be high priced, so you may draw your own conclusions, but as for gold, old Mr. (Lafayette) French was right when he said, "Boys, there's gold in them thar hills, but the men who took it out used a saddle horse and a lariat and branding irons instead of a pick and shovel and gold pan."

Those hills are the greatest cattle country ever, but only a disappointment for a prospector.

Rush Baughn, Rochfort Bridge, Alta.

Two years later a mini–gold rush was started on Big Timber Creek northwest of Morley. Although he was not specifically mentioned in the newspaper article about the discovery, it's possible that King Bearspaw was involved. The original clipping, dated October 1933, is incomplete, but it probably also came from the *Calgary Daily Herald*:

TWENTY-NINE CLAIMS STAKED ALONG

BIG TIMBER CREEK

Calgary, Oct. 8—Gold has been discovered along Big Timber Creek, 65 miles northwest of Morley, Alberta. Fifteen members of the Stoney Indian tribe, in the employ of Harry Ford and Jack Hunter [Chief Sitting Eagle], Calgary Coal operators, arrived in the city Wednesday and immediately filed placer and gold quartz claims at the provincial government land office.

Rich In Gold

The Indians brought with them samples of gravel from Big Timber Creek and the dirt was apparently rich in gold. Mr. Ford produced a phial containing little nuggets and flakes which he claimed he and Mr. Hunter had panned from the creek using an ordinary frying pan.

The samples were assayed at the Technical Institute here and were found to be pure gold.

The Indians were wildly excited over the discovery and the majority of the male members of the tribe have either staked claims or else are going in.

An abandoned cabin and an old prospector's pick were found near the scene of the discovery and the Indians believe that the Lemon Mine famed in song and story will be found in this vicinity.

There is an automobile trail from Calgary to the Eau Claire lumber camp, and the remaining 30 miles to the discovery claim must be negotiated on horseback and pack train. News of the gold find was said to be spreading and many outfits were preparing to go in on Thursday.

For years the Stoneys have hunted in the vicinity of the reported gold strike but it was only this year that they carried out any prospecting work. They first saw the abandoned cabin 35 years ago but no one paid any attention to it until this year when some of the younger members of the tribe explored the ruins and brought to light a rusty old prospector's pick and a gold pan.

In the final analysis, history will judge King Bearspaw. However, it matters little what some have said about him, for he spent more years searching for this hidden Eldorado than any other individual. Such tenacity deserves our respect. Few men keep faith with a dream for over 70 years. It is only fitting that the final word on King Bearspaw and the Lost Lemon Mine should come from Bearspaw himself: "Some people claim that the Lemon Mine exists only in the imagination of old time prospectors and Indian hunters. But I know that is not so. I was just a little boy when I first heard of the Lemon Mine at my mother's knee more than 60 years ago. My grandfather and my father told me about it. They would not lie."

4

The Cast of Characters

THE PASSAGE OF TIME HAS made it difficult to track down detailed, accurate information about most of the major players in the Lost Lemon drama. Census records, newspaper articles and local and oral histories provide clues, but there are few certainties. There is no reliable information as to who was who. The two fragmentary newspaper accounts that survive each give a different name for the central character—the Christian names differ, and the surnames are spelled inconsistently.

Lemon

The prospector Lemon is called by various names in different versions of the Lost Lemon Mine story. This is not surprising, given the nature of the yarn, but the attraction of the tale lies in the intrigue of the murder, the lure of hidden gold and the excitement inherent in trying to unravel a century-old detective tale, not in such humdrum details as Lemon's first name. Yet if we are to find the historic man buried in the legend, it is necessary to examine the few and contradictory references to this mysterious prospector.

In his book *The Range Men*, which was published in 1913, L.V. Kelly writes, "A man named Mark Lemon, at present living in Montana, tells of a prospecting trip he and a party made into the Porcupine Hills in 1869. They found, he declares, placer gold of such exceeding richness that even their hopes were satisfied, but the Blackfeet or Piegans came down and killed all but Lemon, who upon escaping, has never returned, though he still asserts he knows the point where the placer deposits can be found." Significantly, this account puts Lemon in the Porcupine Hills in 1869, one year before he was supposed to have killed Blackjack.

While Kelly describes a prospector named Mark Lemon, Florence Kroesing refers to a Jack Lemmon. Freda Bundy's version of the tale talks of Bill Lemon, and Dan Riley and Neil Nicholson sidestep the difficulty by not referring to Lemon's Christian name at all. This, of course, makes it extremely difficult to decide which Lemon is being discussed in these narratives. The best place to start the search is within the pages of the newspapers of the day. To these newspapers, the story of the Lost Lemon Mine or Lemon

Gulch was just a news story, not an exciting legend told and retold many times. But we must be cautious; even today's newspapers frequently report versions of the news that are at odds with the facts, and such errors are not unique to the 21st century.

The Lemon Gulch story that appeared in the *Calgary Daily Herald* on October 6, 1886, is of little assistance, as it does not mention Lemon's Christian name. The article in the *Helena Daily Rocky Mountain Gazette* on August 6, 1870, gives the name of the prospector as Frank Lemmon. Here, at last, is something that dates from the period and that can be checked. The *Helena Daily Rocky Mountain Gazette* reported that Frank Lemmon was a blacksmith living at the mouth of Cedar Creek in June 1870. This gives us a name, a time and a place—firm clues to the identity of the prospector.

A check of the Montana State Census for the year 1870 reveals that a Ben Lemon was living at Cedar Creek mines. His occupation was listed as mine worker, while his age was given as 37 years. At first, the names Ben Lemon and Frank Lemmon do not appear very similar; however, the microfilm of the original handwritten census document shows Ben Lemon's middle initial as F. Given the American habit of naming sons after deceased statesmen, it seems possible that "Ben F. Lemon" could stand for Benjamin Franklin Lemon, probably known to his friends as Ben or Frank.

The *Helena Daily Rocky Mountain Gazette* also mentions a gentleman named Ben Northington in the article concerning Lemmon. A further check of the original census record shows that Ben Northington was 36 years of age, a mine worker, and that he was listed next to Ben Lemon on the census record. The two men lived in the same domicile, recorded as "Dwelling Number 364." When two people living together shared a common Christian name, often one of them was called by a second Christian name— hence Ben Lemon could have become Frank Lemon. Given the similarity in their ages, their occupations and the fact that they both lived in Cedar Creek in the same dwelling, a strong case can be made that Ben F. Lemon is the Frank Lemmon mentioned in the newspaper article.

There was one other individual named Lemmon living at Cedar Creek. James Lemmon was 51 at the time of the census, and his occupation was listed as "prospecting mines." The census does not list a middle initial for James Lemmon. Could he be our mysterious prospector? The only firm link with the newspaper article is the spelling of his surname. A case could also be made that James Lemmon's occupation, prospecting mines, coincides with what we know of the Lemon who is said to have initially discovered the mine. It is, however, at odds with the newspaper article, which records Lemmon's occupation as blacksmith.

If Ben F. Lemon, who worked in the mines, is our man, then the spelling of his name as reported by the *Gazette* is in error; however, this would hardly have been unusual. Newspapers of the day sometimes spelled names two different ways within a single article, and it would be unwise to rest a case on this evidence. The census does not list a middle initial for prospector James Lemmon, and his occupation does not match the article. While it is difficult to reconcile these minor contradictions, there is a good chance that either James Lemmon or Ben F. Lemon, both residents of Cedar Creek, Montana, could be the man at the heart of the mystery.

The only other man named Lemon or Lemmon in the 1870 Montana Territorial Census is James Lemon, age 25, living in Gallatin County, Bozeman Precinct, Montana. The Montana Territorial Poll list for 1864 shows four men named Lemon or Lemmon living in Madison County: a G. Lemmon living at Virginia City; a J.S. Lemmon living at Junction City Precinct; an F. Lemon living at Virginia City; and an R. Lemon living at Nevada City. There is no historical information that links any of these men to any published account relating to the Lost Lemon Mine story. However, it is possible that R. Lemon, listed as living at Nevada City, may be the Robert H. Lemon mentioned in the papers of Lieutenant James H. Bradley from Fort Benton. Bradley writes of Lemon's arrival at Fort Benton in 1863: "Robert H. Lemon succeeded to the charge of Fort Labarge, which had not been a very profitable business and was destined to bring pecuniary disaster upon its owners." The report goes on to say that Lemon discharged the former agent at Labarge and put his business in the hands of Andrew Dawson, the man who adopted the famous scout Jerry Potts as a young boy.

This may be a very important clue. In the summer of 1862, a package of gold-bearing sand was received by Dawson from Jean L'Heureux, who has been identified as the priest who assisted Lemon in Senator Dan Riley's account. It is possible that in the course of their business relationship at Fort Benton, the gold was mentioned to Robert Lemon by Dawson. If this were the case, perhaps there is a connection between Robert Lemon in Fort Benton, who had learned from Dawson of a golden gulch to the north, and a prospector named Mark Lemon who was seen in the Porcupine Hills in 1869.

There is also a reference to Robert Lemon in *The Mountain Men and the Fur Trade of the Far West*, written by LeRoy R. Hafen. In this book, Ray H. Mattison, of the State Historical Society of North Dakota, mentions Robert Lemon's travels during 1860–61: "Another person who took part in the [trading] venture was Robert Lemon, a clerk in Campbell's St. Louis office. Travelling overland, the partners established two posts on the Upper Missouri: one at Poplar River (Montana), which was operated by Larpenteur and Lemon."

There is little doubt that this is the same Robert Lemon who was involved with the trading company at Fort Benton in 1863. As a partner in quite a large trading company, it is unlikely he would have had time to dash off into the hills, looking for gold. Therefore, it seems reasonable to conclude that Robert Lemon is not directly involved with our story.

Possibly Robert Lemon related the story of L'Heureux's golden sand to a brother or other relative—the prospector seen by Kelly. This would certainly provide the solid link between L'Heureux's gold and the mysterious Lemon and help to tie some of the confusing elements of this story together.

The last newspaper reference to Lemon appeared in the 1886 *Calgary Daily Herald* article "The Lemon Gulch" (see p. 37 for the complete article): "Lemon has, we believe, been seen at the new diggings in the Sweet Grass Hills recently."

History has not recorded the final end of James Lemmon, Ben F. Lemon or Robert Lemon. Is one of them our elusive murderer, or are they merely persons who, by virtue of sharing the name of the central figure in western Canada's most puzzling story, have become themselves a small part of the mystery of the Lost Lemon Mine?

Blackjack

According to Senator Dan Riley's version of the legend, Lemon's unfortunate partner, Blackjack, was the true discoverer of the Cariboo diggings in British Columbia. Using that clue, historian Dr. Hugh Dempsey tracked down a well-known Cariboo prospector named Nehemia T. Smith. According to Dempsey, this individual, who was nicknamed Blackjack, "was born in Maryland. He joined the Fraser River gold rush in 1858 and there started a long partnership with Thomas Latham, also known as 'Dancing Bill.'

He went to the Cariboo the following year and made several fortunes, his most famous strike being in the Blackjack tunnel on Williams Creek in 1862." This information suggests that Nehemia (or Nehemiah) Smith could be the Blackjack involved with the Lost Lemon Mine.

Interestingly, another man named Smith sheds some light on Blackjack's subsequent travels. In his *History of British Columbia*, H.H. Bancroft writes of a man named A.G. Smith:

> A.G. Smith and several others, who in 1866 went to Helena in Montana, worked successfully until August, when an excitement was created about the Saskatchewan diggings [referring to the North Saskatchewan River] which fanned into action the general desire to prospect the eastern slope of the Rocky Mountains, opposite the upper Columbia. Smith set out at once with seven others, for Edmonton, by way of Kootenai Pass, and arrived there safely in thirty-eight days, despite the hostile Indians. The gold deposits were found scattered for a hundred miles above and below Edmonton upon the Saskatchewan bars, but these could be worked only for a short time in the spring and autumn, when the river was low and the yield was nearly two dollars a day or less, with rockers.

On May 2, 1867, the *Victoria Daily Colonist* reprinted an article written by Smith that had first appeared in the *New Westminster British Columbian*. In the article, Smith refers to two well-known Cariboo prospectors named Blackjack and

Dancing Bill, who made a trip to Fort Edmonton searching for gold. This puts Blackjack at Fort Edmonton three years before Lemon made his prospecting trip with a partner bearing this nickname. The Williams Creek Blackjack's familiarity with the country and first-hand knowledge of the gold-bearing gravels on the North Saskatchewan would have been very helpful to Lemon. Smith's article reads as follows:

SASKATCHEWAN AND BIG BEND

The *British Columbian* has conversed with A.G. Smith, who has just arrived from Fort Edmonton on the headwaters of the North Saskatchewan. He went in by way of Vermilion Pass from Blackfoot, and was 38 days in reaching Fort Edmonton. The country is a magnificent open one, dotted with lakes intersected by streams and everywhere covered with the most luxuriant grasses, also abounding in game of all kinds native to this latitude, from prairie chicken, to the grizzly bear and the shaggy buffalo. Winter set in on the 9th of October and Smith and his party remained at the fort, subsisting on fish and rabbits, and the kindness of Mr. Christie, the H.B. Company's agent, at the Fort. The so-called gold mines are confined to the bars of the river, extending so far as is yet known, some 50 miles above and 50 miles below Edmonton. These mines can be worked a few weeks in the spring and a few weeks in the fall of the year, and with rockers, the only machinery yet in use, yield variously 75 cents to $2.50 a day to the hand. The gold is very fine and quicksilver is used in collecting it. There were less than a dozen men mostly half breeds at work. A party of seven including Blackjack and

Dancing Bill, two well known Caribooites, were organizing and fitting out at Edmonton with the view to prospecting the entire country through by Peace River to Cariboo. The Blackfoot Indians are very troublesome, and it is estimated that they have murdered about 300 miners in and about Elk River and Fort Benton Passes, since adventurers have been attracted in that direction. They are a numerous and warlike tribe and openly avow their determination to kill every white man who comes into their country.

It is interesting to note that Smith mentions the hostility of the Blackfoot. This certainly fits with L.V. Kelly's version of the story, wherein Lemon told about Blackfoot or Peigans having massacred his party in the Porcupine Hills two years later.

There is a possibility, but no conclusive evidence, that the Blackjack at Williams Creek was Nehemia Smith. However, there is evidence to dispute Riley's allegation that the Blackjack of Williams Creek and the Blackjack of the Lost Lemon Mine were one and the same man.

The major problem with connecting the two Blackjacks has to do with the timing of the latter's death. Riley stated that Blackjack was murdered by Lemon in 1870 or 1871. If this is true, then the mysterious Blackjack from the Cariboo could not have been Lemon's partner. According to Bancroft, the Williams Creek Blackjack was in Victoria in 1877–78, seven years after he was supposed to have been murdered by Lemon: "Another of the earliest miners on Williams Creek, who became wealthy as the owner of the Black Jack mine, was at Victoria in the winter of 1877–8, dependant on charity for his daily bread."

Admittedly, this individual is not specifically identified as Blackjack, and the company was referred to in the *Cariboo Sentinel* as "Black Jack and Burnes." Thus, there is a possibility that Bancroft is referring to Burnes. However, there can be absolutely no doubt about the article published in the *Victoria Daily Colonist* on July 10, 1883, which reports Blackjack still alive, although in failing health, in a Victoria hospital:

Black Jack—One of the most noted of the Cariboo's early prospectors was an American named "Black Jack." He led the way to many a rich streak of pay dirt and at one time owned rich claims and scattered his dust like a duke. For a long time Black Jack's been an inmate of the hospital, old, sick and decrepit. He has been tenderly cared for and today, with his health somewhat reestablished, is desirous of revisiting his native land. It is therefore hoped that a helping hand will be extended him by citizens generally, so that the poor old pioneer may sail for "home again" by steamer that leaves today.

This is 13 years after Blackjack was supposed to have been murdered; therefore it seems unlikely that the unnamed Blackjack of Williams Creek fame could be the the equally mysterious Blackjack of the Lost Lemon Mine.

The fictional connection between the two may have been made by Jean L'Heureux. On October 9, 1866, L'Heureux visited Fort Edmonton with a party of Bloods who had come to the fort to trade. Since Blackjack and his party also arrived at Edmonton on October 9, it is certain that Blackjack and L'Heureux would have met. Hugh Dempsey has suggested that, given the fact that Senator Dan Riley got his information about the Lost Lemon Mine from his friend Lafayette French, and that French and L'Heureux shared quarters and swapped stories of their days at Blackfoot Crossing, L'Heureux may have embellished the story he had heard from miners in Montana about Lemon and his lost mine. For effect, he may have added Blackjack, the famous prospector from the Cariboo, to give us the bones of the story that survives today.

However, there is a second possibility. In Fred Kennedy's account of Chief Sitting Eagle's story, Jack Lemon and Blackjack are the same person and Dancing Bill is his partner; A.G. Smith's story could also lead to the same conclusion. If that were the case, it's possible that somewhere, in the constant retelling of the legend of the Lost Lemon Mine, someone got the names confused, perhaps placing the nickname "Blackjack" on the wrong individual. "Blackjack" was probably a very common nickname, and there was no shortage of men in the goldfields who called themselves by a variety of names, not wanting their true identities to be known. As a result, we can never know with certainty which Blackjack was being referred to, or if there were multiple Blackjacks in play. Such is the sad lot of the historian.

Another explanation is that Jimmy White's account of the Lost Lemon Mine is correct concerning the name of Lemon's partner and that the Blackjack we are seeking was a man named McGowan. Unfortunately, no information has survived concerning the mysterious McGowan. A search of available records gives no clue to the existence of either McGowan or McIver, the holder of Blackjack's map to the diggings.

Jean L'Heureux

As noted above, the priest associated with Dan Riley's version of the Lost Lemon Mine story is usually identified as Jean L'Heureux, a French Canadian who lived with the Blackfoot and acted as translator to Chief Crowfoot. His name appears with a variety of spellings—Larue, LaRoo or LeRoux—but there is no doubt that the references pertain to one man. While L'Heureux was not an ordained Catholic priest, he nevertheless functioned in this capacity with the Blackfoot, performing weddings and baptisms. L'Heureux came in contact with Lafayette French at Blackfoot Crossing, while working as a translator for Crowfoot.

According to Riley's account, L'Heureux became involved in the Lost Lemon Mine saga when he heard the confession of the half-insane Lemon after he murdered Blackjack. Riley states that this meeting took place at

Tobacco Plains. Here lies one of the problems in the story. The region commonly known as Tobacco Plains has an area of about 20 by 30 miles and lies south of Elko, BC. About one-third of the area is in British Columbia and two-thirds in Montana. It is unclear in the story whether the reference was to Tobacco Plains in general or if it was the name of a specific place. Some believe that the Tobacco Plains referred to in the story was actually the mission at St. Ignatius in Montana or Jocko Mission, south of Flathead in Montana.

There was also a small trading post called Tobacco Plains about one-quarter mile north of the international boundary, consisting of several buildings and the office of the Indian agent for the area. This post was south of the junction of the Elk and the Kootenay rivers and six miles north of the Kootenay Trading Post on the Montana side. Lemon would certainly have travelled this route after leaving the Highwood.

However, there is reason to doubt that the meeting between Lemon and L'Heureux ever took place. Jocko Mission, St. Ignatius and the settlement at Tobacco Plains, given as the possible locations for the meeting, are all well within the territory of the Kootenais, traditional enemies of the Blackfoot, and the following account gives some idea of the state of relations between them.

Near Gleichen, in southern Alberta, lies Squaw Coulee. Charles Short, a pioneer of Spitzee, tells of finding human bones littering the bottom of Squaw Coulee. He was told by the Blackfoot that the shattered bones were all that remained of a party of Kootenais murdered by the Blackfoot. Apparently, a band of Kootenais had been driven from their normal ranges in the Rocky Mountains by deep snow. They cautiously made their way into Blackfoot territory and set up their lodges in Squaw Coulee, hoping to trap buffalo in a nearby pound. The Blackfoot attacked the camp while the hunters were away. On their return, the hunters found the smoking ruins of their burnt teepees and the bodies of their slaughtered women and children.

Given this adversarial relationship, it would have been suicide for the Blackfoot and those closely associated with them to have travelled deep into Kootenai territory to the trading post at Tobacco Plains, Jocko Mission or St. Ignatius. It is also highly unlikely that the Kootenais would have welcomed L'Heureux given his close ties to Crowfoot, their sworn enemy.

The connection between L'Heureux and Lemon may have been made through Lafayette French, who is known to have grubstaked prospectors and traded supplies among the Blackfoot, Stoneys and the Kootenais. The reference to French staking Lemon at Tobacco Plains, coupled with French's friendship with L'Heureux, may provide the key to understanding how the story evolved.

The best documented historical reference tying L'Heureux to rumours of gold is found in the journals written by Lieutenant Bradley when he was stationed at Fort Benton:

Jean L'Heureux (standing) poses with (from left to right) One Spot (Crowfoot's pipe bearer), Blood chief Red Crow and Peigan chief North Axe. GLENBOW ARCHIVES NA-2968-4

In the summer of 1862, a package of sand was received by Dawson (a trader at Benton) from a certain Larue, a pretended priest, who had been living for several years among the Bloods and Blackfeet. Larue sent word with the package that it was gold-bearing sand, taken from a gulch in the north, and that he would guide a party to the locality if desired. The sand was washed at the Fort and was found to contain an astonishing proportion of gold. A party was instantly formed, consisting of Matthew Carroll, James M. Amoux, John Mason Brown (a brother of Gratz Brown of Missouri), a Dr. Atkinson, Paul Longtime, Henry Boswick, Edward Williamson, David Carafel, George Magnum, John Munroe, and _____, which proceeded north in July to prospect. The party pursued a northwesterly course, prospecting upon every stream from the Marias to the Willows, a point about twenty-five miles south of Fort Edmonton, getting a light colour of gold upon every stream, but nothing to justify working. Larue could not be found and the unsuccessful prospectors, after passing the summer in fruitless search, concluded that they had been victimized by the faithless Larue and turned their faces homeward, arriving at Fort Benton in September in such a state of mind that they would have executed summary vengeance on Larue had he fallen into their hands. It is the present belief of Mr. Amoux, shared by others of his associates, that Larue had purposely deceived them by mixing a large quantity of gold dust with the sand and representing this mixture as a fair specimen of the rich fields known to him.

If L'Heureux did in fact mislead the Fort Benton miners in 1862 about rich gold finds in an unnamed gulch, then he certainly could have misled French with stories of gold. This deception might simply have been for the sake of a good yarn, told around the fire in French's post at Blackfoot Crossing.

Perhaps L'Heureux, like French, knew a good story when he heard one, and for the sake of the storyteller's art, altered certain key elements of the tale. Given this, it is certainly possible that French, who was known to have prospected for gold for many years in his travels, may have enthusiastically seized upon L'Heureux's suggestion of a rich gold find in Indian territory. L'Heureux's tale, coupled with Lemon's claim of finding rich diggings, may have been embellished by French to become the Lost Lemon Mine legend. A good campfire story was worth its weight in gold, and it's likely that elements of several different stories have found their way into the surviving accounts.

As a young man, Dan Riley worked for French in High River, so it is almost certain that French was the source of his version of the tale. However, there seems to be no doubt that French himself believed in the Lost Lemon Mine, for he spent the remainder of his life searching for it.

The story of gold diggings, as told by L'Heureux, may have some connection with the following account, which is based upon an article that appeared in *Frontier Guide to Waterton*.

In 1872, a gold strike was reported on the Oldman River. An unnamed Mexican had formed a partnership with a miner from Helena, Montana, who had located a rich deposit of gold. Together with a third miner, they made their way into Canada as far north as the Oldman River. Apparently the diggings were quite rich, for within a short time they had taken $1,200 in coarse gold from along the banks of the river.

The country surrounding the Oldman River was within the territory controlled by the Blackfoot, who were very hostile to any whites travelling across their lands. Eventually, the miners were attacked by the Blackfoot, and two of them were killed. The Mexican, although severely wounded, managed to hide the gold and to escape with his life.

Arriving at Fort Benton after recuperating from his wounds, the Mexican attempted to form a new party in an effort to recover his gold. He eventually joined up with a group of whisky traders who were heading north into Canada. Again, misfortune struck his venture, for the traders fell into the clutches of the NWMP, and everyone was promptly arrested. The Mexican told his story to the constables at Fort Macleod, promising to exchange the gold for his release. When the NWMP investigated the scene of the massacre, the bones of the two miners were found, along with burned remnants of wagons, tents and harness. But no gold was ever found.

The Mexican was returned to Fort Macleod and imprisoned for his involvement in the whisky trade. When spring came, he managed to escape from the stockade but was never able to return for his lost gold. Sometime later, he was found dead on the prairie with a bullet in his body.

Is there a connection between this tale of gold on the Oldman River and a story of rich gold diggings in the country of the Blackfoot, as told by L'Heureux to the miners of Fort Benton? Perhaps the answer lies with the bones of a nameless Mexican.

There is one more piece of information that may throw new light on the motives of the bogus priest. In his journals, immediately following the denunciation of L'Heureux, Lieutenant Bradley records an opinion expressed by I.G. Baker, head of the I.G. Baker Company.

> Mr. I.G. Baker suggested another interpretation, and time must determine which is the true one. He thinks that Larue may have sent honest dust, and really intended to guide a party to rich gold fields known to him in the ranges of the Indians with whom he lived, but that witnessing the sudden influx of hundreds of white men to the more southern diggings as soon as they became known, and fearing a similar rush into his own country, he repented of his promise and kept out of the way of the party.

We have no way of knowing if I.G. Baker was correct in his assumption. Whatever the verdict of history, only Jean L'Heureux knew the truth about his gold. If L'Heureux was largely responsible for creating the legend of the Lost Lemon Mine, it was only because those who came after him wanted to believe it. L'Heureux settled in Pincher Creek from 1892 to 1912, but little more is known of him. Eventually, he entered the Lacombe Home in Midnapore, just south of Calgary, and died completely destitute in 1919.

Lafayette French

History has left us no photographs of Lafayette French. Like Lemon and Blackjack, he is known to us only as a faceless figure trapped within the fabric of a century-old mystery. French was born in Pennsylvania in about 1840 and worked for the Standard Oil Company before coming west, where he worked as a buffalo hunter, independent trader, prospector and, in his later years, as a cattleman. He first came to Alberta in the early 1880s. As an independent trader, French had no loyalties to anyone but himself, and it is certain there was no love lost between him and the I.G. Baker Company, which would have preferred to have a monopoly on trade with the Plains tribes. The Natives, realizing that it was in their best interest to trade with several groups of whites, always tried to play one trader off against another. And, like any other trader, French overcharged the Natives when he could and underpaid them if the opportunity presented itself. But French did enjoy one advantage in dealing with the Blackfoot that his competitors did not: some years earlier he had saved the life of Crowfoot, their chief. The incident is chronicled in L.V. Kelly's *The Range Men*:

> French and other traders, trading at High River, were surrounded by a large number of trafficking red men, and among them was Crowfoot, who came to French's cabin to rest. One of the traders was unpopular with Crowfoot, and

consequently lost considerable Blackfoot business, much to his annoyance. Thinking to remove the cause of his ban, this man filled a brave with firewater and told him to go and shoot Crowfoot in French's cabin. The savage followed directions as far as going to the door of the shack, drawing a bead on Crowfoot's head and pressing the trigger. But, as he pressed, Lafayette French came around the corner, saw the state of affairs at a glance, and swung the rifle muzzle upward as it exploded, the ball crashing harmlessly into the mud roof. Crowfoot never forgot this act, and continued to repay while he lived.

The connection between Lafayette French, Crowfoot and Jean L'Heureux is very important to our understanding of the story of the Lost Lemon Mine as told by Dan Riley. It was surely through Crowfoot that L'Heureux and French met at Blackfoot Crossing. There is also a reference to French and a Father LaRue at Blackfoot Crossing in *The Range Men*:

French, or, as he was afterwards named in the Blackfoot tongue, "The Lifted Arm," built a shack at Blackfoot Crossing and proceeded to take advantage of his popularity (as a result of having saved the life of Chief Crowfoot). Other traders, feeling jealous of him, are said to have entered unofficially into a conspiracy with certain of the Mounted Police to discredit him with whites and savages alike. Two women were to enter French's store, and then commence screaming, whereupon the Mounted Police were to rush the place and arrest French on charge of a serious crime. Crowfoot heard of it, and, telling French, planned a counter-plot. Two

Catholic priests, Father laRue and Father Scollen, were very popular among the Blackfoot, and it was arranged with one of these men to hide himself in the store and come out at the psychological moment. The day came, and with it the squaws arrived and commenced to scream as per program. The thunder of horses hoofs indicated the arrival of the police, the thunder of heavy fists on the door and the roar of a voice demanding admittance in the name of the Queen indicated that the stage setting was reaching the climax. French opened the door as ordered, and the policeman who stormed in was confronted not only by French and two cowed squaws, but also by the Roman Catholic priest in his churchly garments. The plot died a sudden death and was not resurrected.

While Kelly does not specify whether Father Scollen or Jean L'Heureux was the priest used to foil the plot against French, it is virtually certain that L'Heureux at least knew of it. Given the nature of L'Heureux's position as translator for Crowfoot, it seems highly probable that L'Heureux would have been asked to render assistance to the friend who had saved Crowfoot's life.

According to Dan Riley's version of the legend, French spent the remainder of his life trying to find the lost mine after receiving a crude map drawn by Lemon himself. Unfortunately, it is not possible to state with any certainty whether or not such a map ever existed. But if it did, it is clear that French believed that it was genuine.

The final mention of French in *The Range Men* corroborates Riley's account of his death:

The ruins of Lafayette French's cabin in the Crowsnest Pass.
BOB CANTIN

Lafayette French, the old trader, friend of Crowfoot, and one of the first white men in the west in its wildest days, came to an unfortunate end about Christmas of 1912. He had been living for some time up High River in a small cabin owned by George Emmerson. He was an old, feeble man, and in some unknown way his cabin took fire, burning completely, and so badly injuring French, that though he escaped to the prairie and was there picked up, he passed away in the High River Hospital a short time later.

No doubt French, who we are told was an outrageous storyteller, would be most gratified to know that his stories of the Lost Lemon Mine were still inspiring people to search the mountains for Lemon's lost treasure decades later. While French's face has been lost to the past, his story and quest for the Lost Lemon Mine have become part of the lore of the Canadian West.

George Emmerson

George Emmerson was born in 1841 and raised in Danville, Quebec. As a young man, Emmerson headed west, homesteading in Iowa. In 1868, he first came to what was then known as the Northwest Territory. Attracted by rumours of gold, Emmerson and his party crossed the border south of Medicine Hat and made their way north to the North Saskatchewan River. The following winter, Emmerson worked for the HBC at Fort Edmonton, driving dog teams and hauling freight between Fort Garry and Fort Edmonton, a trip of over 1,000 miles.

Emmerson spoke both the Cree and Blackfoot languages fluently, skills he no doubt acquired on the long freighting trips between Fort Garry and Fort Edmonton. The crews of these freight brigades were a mix of whites, Metis and Natives who often spent their time gambling, drinking, fighting and whooping it up. These wild times with the HBC served Emmerson well, for it was said that as a free trader he lived among the Natives on little more than wild berries, buffalo tongues and wild duck eggs.

After the NWMP arrived, Emmerson sold cattle to the Mounties and freighted supplies from the HBC fort at Edmonton for the building of a new fort at Calgary. In 1876, Emmerson brought in a herd of cattle from Montana to the NWMP at Fort Macleod. This was the first of many such cattle drives, and it was probably through these dealings that Emmerson and Lafayette French became friends. In 1879, Tom Lynch and Emmerson brought in 1,000 head of cattle from Montana and settled on the north side of the Highwood River, about four miles west of the present town of High River.

Emmerson spent much time in his later years searching for the Lost Lemon Mine. A prospector all his life, Emmerson would often slip away into the mountains with French for weeks at a time, scouring the coulees and passes for the elusive treasure. In his later years, George Emmerson divided his time between High River and his ranch in the Sand Hills, where he died in September 1920, after a short illness.

Kootenai Brown

John George Brown was born in Ennistymon, County Clare, Ireland, on September 13, 1839. Arriving in the Wild Horse Creek area in the summer of 1865, Brown worked as a trapper, miner and special constable. When rumours of a rich gold strike on the North Saskatchewan circulated through the camps, Brown made his way north to Fort Edmonton, through the South Kootenay Pass. Brown was taken with the wild splendour of the country and vowed to return. He finally settled in the Waterton Lakes area and teamed up with notorious whisky trader Fred Kanouse to conduct a thriving business from a crude shack near the present site of the Prince of Wales Hotel. It was during this period, while trading furs with the Kootenais, that Brown earned the nickname "Kootenai."

While Brown's base of operations was in Waterton Lakes, he travelled to Fort Benton and to Fort Macleod to trade and almost certainly met Lafayette French during these expeditions. Both French and Brown prospected for oil and were involved in a joint venture with A.P. Patrick, a surveyor with the Dominion government. While it is not certain if Brown spent much time searching for the Lost Lemon Mine, a story that appeared in *Frontier Guide to Waterton* may be connected to the mine.

In September 1892, Brown delivered a sample of ore to the assay office in Fort Macleod, stating that he discovered it in a rock outcrop at 4,000 feet. When the sample was analyzed, it was found to contain gold, silver and copper in an ore of lead known as galena. When others learned of his gold find and asked Brown about the locality of the strike, he promptly forgot where he had found it. This led to the assumption that the rock samples had come from the Waterton vicinity, and Brown did not want a gold rush to ruin the splendour of his Waterton Lakes.

Even if this sample did not come from the Lost Lemon Mine—the rock type is different from the sample described by the traders at Fort Benton, Montana—it seems to prove that gold was present in the rocks around Waterton Lakes and lends credence to reports of gold found to the north along the eastern slopes of the Rockies.

The remainder of Brown's days were spent around Waterton Lakes, where he lived with his Cree wife, Blue Flash of Lightning, in a small cabin. In 1895, the Dominion government created a 54-square-mile reserve around the Waterton Lakes and appointed Brown as game warden and fisheries inspector. In May 1911, the Kootenay Forest Reserve became Waterton Lakes National Park. Brown remained as forest ranger, still patrolling the park on his old buckskin pony, clad in white chaps and waist sash, until his retirement in 1914 at age 75. His health began to fail by the summer of 1916 and he moved to Cardston to get medical assistance. The colourful story of Kootenai Brown came to a close with his death on July 18, 1916.

John Nelson

John Nelson was an old-time buffalo hunter and trader who settled in the North Fork country in the 1860s. In 1868, Nelson was heading into the foothills with a party of prospectors to search for gold. The prospectors lost a pair of pliers in a creek, which they then named Pincher Creek. In later years, Nelson was convinced he knew the location of the Lost Lemon Mine and spent the final years of his life hunting for this elusive prize.

Nelson died on November 12, 1907. It is reported that

the dimensions of his coffin were based upon a rough estimate of his size rather than an actual measurement. It turned out that the coffin was a tad on the small side, and Nelson had to be stuffed into the box before he could be hauled away to the Livingstone Cemetery. This insult was compounded while his coffin was being moved up the hill to the cemetery in the back of an open-ended wagon. As the procession climbed the hill, the coffin began to slide out of the wagon. Nelson's son-in-law, who was following behind in a democrat, hollered to the driver, "Look out! The old son of a bitch is getting away."

Apparently Nelson was interred without further incident.

Bill Olin

Bill Olin was one of the original settlers in the North Fork country and first came to the Pincher Creek area in the early 1870s with a party of traders, Natives and buffalo hunters coming north from Montana. Olin, John Nelson and Matt Holloway settled for a time near La Grandeur's Crossing on the Oldman River, then moved to the North Fork country or Livingstone district. Later, Olin married and moved up the creek that now bears his name, close to the spot where it enters the North Fork.

Olin spent much of his time seeking the Lost Lemon Mine. He shared Nelson and Holloway's opinion that Lemon had secreted his gold in the Gap, and that the treasure was a cache of stolen gold from the goldfields near Fort Steele, rather than from an actual mine.

It was reported that Olin died about 1906 as a result of a final binge after having been warned by his doctor that he would have to stop drinking. In a state of intoxication, Olin froze his legs, which resulted in complications that killed him shortly afterward. He was survived by his wife and three children.

5

Anatomy
of a Mystery

THE PRECEDING CHAPTERS PRESENT all the available evidence concerning the Lost Lemon Mine. While every attempt has been made to authenticate the original material, no definitive judgments can be made concerning the veracity of these sources. Even though the accounts were presented as the truth, many have been twisted and confused over time, and some may be totally false. In spite of these limitations, a detailed examination of some of these stories can provide the reader with insights concerning this historical mystery.

The Prospector Stories
Dan Riley's account of the Lost Lemon Mine seems to have a

number of historical flaws; these have been discussed in the sections dealing with Lafayette French and Jean L'Heureux in Chapter 4. Even considering these shortcomings, however, the story appears to contain some of the answers to the puzzle of Lemon's lost mine—and suggests that clues may be found in the Crowsnest Pass.

The Crowsnest Pass, mentioned in Riley's version and most of the other Lost Lemon Mine stories, contains an ancient lava flow that extends from south of the Crowsnest River north to Racehorse Creek. These unusual rocks, known as the Crowsnest Volcanics, are the remnants of an outpouring of lava from a volcanic vent or series of vents that flanked the eastern slopes of the rising Rockies about 100 million years ago. What makes these lava flows interesting is that under certain conditions such rocks have been known to host metals. Usually, the metals are iron or copper, but sometimes volcanics contain traces of gold. While the concentrations of gold in the lavas are too low to make them useful for mining, sometimes this gold can be transported by solutions of hot, acidic water associated with volcanic eruption.

Under normal conditions, gold does not dissolve in water. However, if water is hot enough and acidic enough, it is capable of forming solutions of gold. There is a great deal of water associated with a volcanic eruption; most of the gas cloud from an erupting volcano is steam. While the gold in the lava is invisible to the naked eye, it can travel in solution a great distance from the original volcanic rocks. If the chemistry of the water changes, the gold it is carrying may be precipitated and deposited. This means that a case can be made for the Lost Lemon Mine being located somewhere along this strip of volcanic rocks.

The most common rocks found on the eastern slopes of the Rockies are limestones, also called carbonates, since they contain calcium carbonate. Calcium carbonate is used in antacid products to reduce the amount of stomach acid. When acidic solutions of water carrying gold come in contact with limestones, the acidity of the water is lowered, which causes the gold to come out of solution and be deposited in the limestone.

Most of the Crowsnest Pass is limestone, including Turtle Mountain, the source of the huge slide that destroyed the town of Frank in 1903. The rocks of the Crowsnest Volcanics outcrop in the vicinity of these limestones. While the Crowsnest Volcanics do not lie directly in contact with limestones on the surface, the rocks of the Blairmore Formation, which underlie the Crowsnest, are thought to contain clastics or fragments of limestone or calcareous material. Also, it should be noted that volcanic plugs formed from the lava that fed the volcanic eruptions pass through older limestones that may be as much as 5,000 feet thick in places.

While it is difficult to state exactly what contacts exist between the Crowsnest Volcanics and carbonates, it is possible that such a geological relationship may have caused the formation of bonanza gold deposits at these contacts or within the volcanics themselves. Bonanza deposits are very rare but may be responsible for localized pockets of extremely rich gold ore. If gold-bearing solutions were present during the eruptive phase of the Crowsnest Volcanics, these contact sites must be considered prime candidates for bonanza gold deposits.

Geological explorations conducted by the author and Bob Cantin in December 1988 provided the first evidence of the presence of gold. A number of samples collected that winter showed elevated gold values in pyrites extracted from the Crowsnest Volcanics. This suggests that Lemon and Blackjack could have found a bonanza deposit, either in the Crowsnest Volcanics or along its margins. These deposits may have occupied a very small area, and unless they were uncovered by accident, as in the case of Lemon and Blackjack, they might never be found again, as carbonates are not normally associated with gold deposits. It is only in recent years, with much higher gold prices and modern methods of geochemical prospecting, that volcanic formations such as the Crowsnest Volcanics are beginning to be explored. It is worth emphasizing that even though the elevated gold values we found in our examination of the volcanics support the theory of a possible bonanza deposit, they were well below any values that could ever be mined at a profit.

Old-time prospectors can certainly be excused if they did not find gold in the Crowsnest Pass. The traditional method of testing pyrites for gold was to crush the rock and pan the crushed material, looking for visible gold. What makes the gold in the Crowsnest Volcanics so difficult to detect using traditional prospecting techniques is that it is locked up in the crystals of iron pyrite at the molecular level; that is, atoms of gold are hidden in the lattice of the iron pyrite crystal. Such gold has been termed "invisible gold."

In Riley's account, Crowsnest Lake was the location where Lemon and the party of prospectors were to rendez-vous with John McDougall, the Metis who found and buried Blackjack's body. Crowsnest Lake is only about two miles west of the Crowsnest Volcanics. The rocks of this formation run north and south in a narrow strip along the western side of the Livingstone Range. They cross the Crowsnest River where the town of Coleman is located today and extend north with outcrops where Racehorse and Dutch creeks cut across this narrow strip of volcanic rocks. Both these creeks are mentioned in several of the Lost Lemon Mine stories.

While Racehorse Creek is not specifically mentioned in Riley's story, he states that a man named Nelson accompa-nied Lemon on the trip back from Tobacco Plains to search for the diggings. This was almost certainly John Nelson, mentioned by both Bundy and Nicholson. Riley goes on to say that Nelson left Crowsnest Lake and headed north to search for the Lost Lemon Mine. This route would have taken him up toward the headwaters of Racehorse Creek. To the east of this location, Racehorse Creek cuts into the Crowsnest Volcanics, and the possibility of a bonanza deposit along the margins of the lava flows cannot be discounted. If there is any truth to the prospector stories of Lemon and Blackjack striking gold in the Livingstone Range, then the rocks of the Crowsnest Volcanics would be the likely source in this other-wise unlikely geological setting.

Freda Bundy's account provides further evidence to sup-port the bonanza-deposit theory. Bundy said that Bill Olin, William Lee and Biggs, a trapper from Montana, travelled past the Whispering Gates of the North Fork and farther back into the mountains while searching for Lemon's cabin. The first major creek on the North Fork past the Whispering Gates is Dutch Creek, which also cuts through the rocks of the Crowsnest Volcanics and, like Racehorse Creek, could be a site of bonanza gold deposits.

Freda Bundy also wrote that there may have been a connection between the old First Nations trail that ran up Racehorse Creek and Lemon's gold. The trail leads through the Racehorse Pass, finally connecting with the Elk River north of Sparwood.

There is a very important connection between Sparwood and Florence Kroesing's account of Ay-Ko-Skun and the Lost Lemon Mine. Kroesing states that after killing Lemon's partner, Ay-Ko-Skun and her son spent a number of days in the bush, travelling through strange country before emerging near the present location of Sparwood. If Kroesing's account is correct, then the pair's probable route would have taken them into the Livingstone Range. It is not possible to state with any certainty if they travelled west along Dutch or Racehorse creeks, but both creeks are possible sites for bonanza deposits, which would fit with the story told by Ay-Ko-Skun. Indeed, the headwaters of Racehorse Creek are only about 12 miles from Sparwood.

This is one possible interpretation of Ay-Ko-Skun's journey to Sparwood; however, the evidence could also point in a different direction. After Ay-Ko-Skun killed Lemon's partner, she and her son travelled "high into the mountains in a westerly direction." Later, she supposedly lost her bearings, but eventually arrived at the present site of Sparwood.

If one supposes for a moment that their direction of travel was east instead of west, the location of Lemon's cabin and the mine may have been west of the Elk River and in the East Kootenays rather than on the eastern slopes of the Rockies. This would agree with the account of the Lost Lemon Mine as told by Neil Nicholson and Jimmy White, which put Lemon's lost mine in the East Kootenay district.

There is at least one powerful argument in favour of the East Kootenay theory. It is reasonable to assume that Ay-Ko-Skun would have fled in an easterly direction after she had murdered Lemon's partner, for she came from the Blood Reserve near Cardston, Alberta. It would be unusual for a woman with a young child to flee west when the safety of her home tribe and reserve lay in the opposite direction.

In addition, it seems highly unlikely that Ay-Ko-Skun would have been lost in either the Livingstone Range or the Crowsnest Pass; her people and other tribes in the area have been using the Crowsnest Pass and the other mountain passes for thousands of years. It is certainly possible that she was heading east into the Crowsnest Pass from the East Kootenays when she arrived at Sparwood.

The fact that Ay-Ko-Skun's story takes place in the 1890s is a discrepancy that cannot be reconciled with the information available to us at this long remove. It is certain that the Lemon stories for which we have written evidence took place some 20 years earlier. This raises the possibility that Ay-Ko-Skun's husband was not Lemon but another prospector whose name has been lost to us. Perhaps similarities between the Ay-Ko-Skun and earlier Lost Lemon Mine stories caused the name of the more-famous Lemon to be attached to the later story. Mrs. Kroesing was repeating the tale as it was told to her, and like much of the folklore that has come down to us, the details have blurred over time; however, the details of Ay-Ko-Skun's story, dates aside, dovetail so neatly with other aspects of the Lemon story that it is impossible to overlook her account.

The Desperado Stories

Most of the desperado stories place the source of Lemon's

gold in the East Kootenay region of BC. Neil Nicholson's informants—Bill Olin, John Nelson, Matt Holloway and William Lee—stated that Lemon and Blackjack might have worked a claim in the Kootenay country of BC, but that there were also stories that they had hijacked the gold and were heading to Fort Benton when Lemon murdered Blackjack. Another pioneer, Sam Livingstone, also believed that Lemon and Blackjack could have been desperadoes.

Nicholson's account seems to date the Lost Lemon Mine story to sometime between 1864 and 1873. As the Wild Horse Creek gold rush was still in full swing during 1864, the story of the Lost Lemon Mine may have taken place during 1863–64, when Kootenai Brown was serving as a constable on Wild Horse Creek. Although Brown left Wild Horse Creek in 1864, gold mining still continued there for many years after the rush was over. It would certainly be reasonable to assume that as long as they were mining gold, miners were being robbed in the Wild Horse country.

If Lemon and Blackjack did conspire to murder and rob the miners, then it seems they were successful. But stealing gold at the point of a gun and keeping it are two different things entirely. If Nicholson's account is correct and Lemon hid his gold in the Gap, then it is most certainly still there.

Men in desperate situations frequently resort to hiding their treasure with the expectation of returning one day to collect their prize. Perhaps Lemon hurriedly buried his gold and failed to correctly mark its location on his map.

Landmarks change over time—trees fall down or sandbars vanish as rivers change their course—and the human memory is very unreliable. A frantically scribbled map could turn out to be more of a hindrance than a help if a miner failed to notice all the tiny details in the lay of the land in his haste to escape.

If this is indeed what happened to Lemon in the Gap, then he is not alone in his misfortune. The following tale tells of another sack of gold that slipped away during the gold rush on Wild Horse Creek.

A party of prospectors who had done very well on Wild Horse Creek were heading south down the Kootenay River carrying their gear and gold to Washington State, where they planned to rest up and spend the winter in more civilized surroundings. Before they reached the border, however, a First Nations war party appeared on the banks of the river. The frightened miners took to their paddles with a fury, hoping to outrun the war party, which was galloping along the banks. The miners were able to beach their raft near Tobacco Plains on the west bank of the Kootenay River. With the war party fast approaching from across the river, the miners quickly buried their gold. They were not able to escape in time and all but one of them were killed. The lone survivor was a man named McAndrews, who was left for dead. It is said that McAndrews later died in Walla Walla, Washington, but before his death, he managed to draw a map for his son, showing the location of the hidden treasure. His son spent many summers in a fruitless search for the lost gold. To this day, it is unknown whether the First Nations attackers found it, or more likely, like Lemon's gold, it still lies hidden.

Was the Lemon-Blackjack situation similar? Did Lemon and Blackjack steal the gold from the miners of Wild Horse Creek and hide a saddlebag of nuggets in the Gap? It is certainly compelling evidence that John Nelson and Matt Holloway continued to search the Gap for Lemon's gold 20 years after it was said to have been hidden.

It is worthy of note that many old maps of the area also list the Crowsnest Pass as "The Gap." While this is extremely thin evidence, it is possible that this was the gap searched by Nelson and Holloway, and it should not be ruled out in our hunt for the location of the Lost Lemon Mine.

When someone mentions the East Kootenay district, they are usually referring to the area surrounding Fort Steele and the Wild Horse Creek gold rush. Several of the Lost Lemon Mine stories, including those written by Freda Bundy and Neil Nicholson, report that the old-timers said Lemon's gold may have come from the East Kootenay area. But it seems there are two East Kootenays. One is in the area of Fort Steele; the other was a former locality listed on some maps of the Crowsnest Pass and located on the eastern end of Crowsnest Lake. It seems to have been named East Kootenay sometime in the 1890s. While it is not possible to state with any certainty exactly what the old-timers told Freda Bundy and Neil Nicholson around the turn of the century, it is possible that it was this Crowsnest-area East Kootenay to which they were referring when speaking of Lemon's lost gold.

If this were the case, it would agree with other accounts that placed the Lost Lemon Mine in the vicinity of the Crowsnest Pass. Crowsnest Lake was mentioned as a meeting place for Lemon and the prospectors. Racehorse Creek and Dutch Creek, both suggested as possible locations for the Lost Lemon Mine, are just a few miles to the north.

Fred Kennedy's account from Chief Sitting Eagle concludes that Lemon and Dancing Bill were outlaws from the East Kootenay region of British Columbia. Chief Bearspaw and his people were suspicious of Lemon for several reasons. The first of these was Lemon's assertion that the gold he traded for new horses came from a "mine" that he claimed to have found. The Stoneys knew this to be untrue, for they recognized the nuggets Lemon offered in trade as being from a placer deposit. Given the fact that Lemon lied about his gold, perhaps his version of events leading up to the shooting death of his partner, Dancing Bill, was also untrue. Coupled with the fact that Lemon and Dancing Bill attempted a winter crossing of the high mountain passes, this evidence seemed to point toward their involvement in some criminal undertaking.

Chief Jacob Bearspaw knew of no gold on the eastern slopes of the Rockies; therefore, it seemed reasonable for him to assume that Lemon's nuggets came from BC. If they had been legitimately earned by Lemon and Dancing Bill, there would have been no need for them to risk their lives in a winter crossing of the pass, unless they were incredibly stupid. While this was possible, it is evident that Chief Bearspaw didn't believe it.

Jimmy White's account is also emphatic in its judgment of Lemon and Blackjack being nothing more than bandits and bushwhackers. While it is not possible to say if any of the stories are true, a number of details of White's version correlate nicely with those in other accounts.

White mentions that Lemon had a cabin up a creek on one of the rivers within 15 miles of Fort Steele. This information could point toward either Wild Horse Creek or the Bull River. As discussed above, Ay-Ko-Skun's journey through the mountains ended at Sparwood, which could indicate that she and her son were fleeing from Lemon's murder in BC's East Kootenay region. This would fit very well with White's assertion that Lemon's cabin was in this vicinity. If one supposes that the cabin was somewhere along the Bull River, then Ay-Ko-Skun might have travelled up the Bull River and through the Hartley Pass, hitting the Elk River several miles south of Sparwood.

Both White and Ay-Ko-Skun mention that the gold was buried in a hole in the cabin floor. Ay-Ko-Skun claimed she removed the gold from the cabin and buried it with Lemon's body at the diggings. Again, this correlates with White's assertion that the gold had been dug up long ago, and would certainly account for the fact that White expressed little interest in searching for Lemon's gold, even though he had a map that would lead him to the prospector's cabin.

The First Nations Stories

Art Cantin's account and Colin Thompson's story both tell a tale of the mysterious red gold that was seen at the Red Lodge trading post in 1894, or just before the turn of the 20th century. While it is not possible to say if there is a direct correlation between the Red Lodge stories and the gold of the Lost Lemon Mine, many people are of the opinion that such a connection exists.

The last First Nations story, which chronicles King Bearspaw's lifelong search for the Lost Lemon Mine, requires no explanation. There can be little doubt that whatever others might have said about the mine being no more than a will-o'-the-wisp, King Bearspaw never lost faith in his vision.

Epilogue

IN 1989, THERE WAS A mini–gold rush in the Crowsnest Pass when news leaked out that gold had been found in the Crowsnest Volcanics. The newspapers and other media that covered the story gave the impression that the streets of the Crowsnest Pass were literally paved with gold, but the reality was not quite so exciting.

If Lemon and Blackjack did indeed find gold, the deposit they stumbled upon that day long ago is still waiting to be found by some lucky prospector. The more recent gold discoveries in the Crowsnest Pass merely suggest that the old stories about the lost mine and the golden treasure on the eastern slopes of the Rockies could be true.

Over the last three decades, I have always heard the same

questions: "Do you know where the gold is?" or "Are you a bil-lionaire yet?" or "Aren't you excited that you've discovered the Lost Lemon Mine?" I smile and answer that I am still poor, and that I did not, in fact, find the Lost Lemon Mine, but it usually makes little difference to the people asking the questions. Gold does funny things to people, and I suppose folks have always been fascinated with the idea of finding lost riches.

When the conversation turns to stories of hidden gold mines or buried treasures, people are excited to share their own stories. Human nature being what it is, everyone wants to contribute something to our oral history. What grand-parent or old-timer can resist the temptation of an eager audience who calls for yet another exciting tale of the good old days? No doubt the desire to tell a tale of mystery or lost treasure has been ingrained in our psyche since the days when oral history and legends were passed from generation to generation over a smoking campfire.

I am not dismissing any of the Lost Lemon Mine stories; there is certainly a grain of truth in all of them. I am sure that each teller of the tale repeated it to the best of his or her ability, but when memory fails, storytellers have a tendency to improvise. Even without intending to mislead the audi-ence, they may fabricate details, and after a few repetitions, these new "facts" become indistinguishable from the origi-nal story. The audience cannot know what is truth and what is fiction, yet they are the people who will repeat the tale to their own children, perhaps years later.

I am frequently asked if I have a favourite Lost Lemon Mine story. I do not, for I think all of them offer some insights into the legend. The fact that I found evidence of gold in the Crowsnest Pass does not mean that all the other stories should be rejected. Jimmy White at Fort Steele believed Lemon and Blackjack were thieves and scoundrels who robbed the miners of the Wild Horse. Perhaps they did. Perhaps all the stories of the trappers and the mining camps are based on real events. King Bearspaw and all the others who searched the mountains for Lemon's lost mine undoubtedly believed they were on the trail of the golden bonanza.

The discoveries in the Crowsnest Pass are not the end of the story of the Lost Lemon Mine but a new beginning. Using modern methods unknown to Lemon and Blackjack, prospectors are once again going into the mountains around the Crowsnest Pass to search for gold.

As the years pass, I feel a close kinship with the men who searched the mountains looking for the lost Eldorado. Given the publicity generated by the 1989 gold rush in the Crowsnest Pass, the story of the Lost Lemon Mine will survive another 100 years or more. The mystery of the Lost Lemon Mine is a part of Canadian history that should never be forgotten, and I hope this book helps to keep the legend alive. It is too full of drama and mystery to pass out of our collective consciousness. Perhaps others will follow my lead and pick up the trail where I have left off, and maybe one day some clever soul will put it all together.

Bibliography

Albertan. November 11, 1961.

Anderson, Frank. *Frontier Guide to Waterton, Land of Leisure.* Calgary: Frontier Publishing, 1968.

Bancroft, Hubert H. *History of British Columbia 1792–1887.* San Francisco: The History Company, 1887.

Bradley, James H. Papers. Montana Historical Society Archives. Helena, MT.

Calgary Daily Herald. October 6, 1886; February 16, 1931; March 6, 1931; November 9, 1961.

Crowsnest Pass Historical Society. *Crowsnest and Its People.* Coleman, AB: Crowsnest Pass Historical Society, 1979.

Hafen, LeRoy H., ed. *The Mountain Men and the Fur Trade of the Far West.* 10 vols. Glendale, CA: Arthur H. Clark Co., 1965–72.

Helena Daily Rocky Mountain Gazette. "The Stampede to the Flathead Country." August 6, 1870.

Inwood, Damian. *Fort Steele: The Golden Era.* Langley, BC: Sunfire Publications, 1986.

Kelly, L.V. *The Range Men.* Toronto: William Briggs, 1913.

Kennedy, Fred. *Alberta Was My Beat.* Calgary: The Albertan, 1975.

Kroesing, Florence. "Ay-Ko-Skun and the Lost Lemon Mine." *Lethbridge Herald.* January 5, 1960.

Nicholson, Neil. Papers. Sheilagh S. Jameson fonds, Series 4, Glenbow Foundation Papers 1935–74, M-8119-202.

Primrose, Tom. *Nanton News*. July 24, 1959.

Riley, Dan, Tom Primrose, and Hugh Dempsey. *The Lost Lemon Mine*. Surrey, BC: Heritage House, 1980.

Riley, Daniel E. "The Lost Lemon Mine." *Alberta Folklore Quarterly 2*, No. 1 (March 1946).

Smith, A.G. "Saskatchewan and Big Bend." *Victoria Daily Colonist*. May 2, 1867.

Wood, Kerry. *A Corner of Canada*. Red Deer, AB: privately printed, 1966.

Index

137

Acknowledgements

I could not have completed this book without the assistance of a wide variety of people, who gave generously of their time, their memories and their support. I particularly want to thank my friend Bob Cantin, whose stories of his father's search for the Lost Lemon Mine were invaluable; my dear friend, the late Garth Milvain, who grew up in Lafayette French's cabin in the Crowsnest Pass, and who always believed in the project; my very patient editor, Lesley Reynolds, who helped impose order on historical chaos; and, finally, with love, my wife, Michelle, who has listened to this story for the last 25 years and has always provided expert assistance with a smile.

About the Author

Ron Stewart has written several books on historical and geological topics. A native of Alberta, he worked for 15 years with the University of Alberta's Department of Earth and Atmospheric Sciences before becoming a consultant. His career has involved a series of exploits, including jumping out of helicopters in remote areas of northern British Columbia; diving to a Spanish wreck off the coast of Florida; and encountering bears in the Yukon, mountain lions in the Blue Ridge Mountains and black widow spiders and copperhead snakes in North Carolina. Currently, Ron has several television and writing projects underway, including historical non-fiction and two works of fiction. Ron lives happily with his wife of 42 years, Michelle, an old grey cat named Maggie and 400 metric tons of books.

More Great Books in the Amazing Stories Series

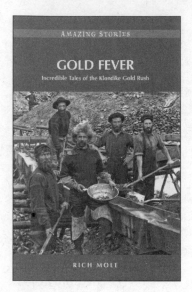

Gold Fever

Incredible Tales of the
Klondike Gold Rush

Rich Mole

(ISBN 978-1-894974-69-1)

In 1897, tens of thousands of would-be prospectors flooded into the
Yukon in search of instant wealth during the Klondike Gold Rush.
In this historical tale of mayhem and obsession, characters like
prospectors George Carmack and Skookum Jim, Skagway gangster
Soapy Smith and Mountie Sam Steele come to life. Enduring savage
weather, unforgiving terrain, violence and starvation, a lucky few made
their fortune, and some just as quickly lost it. The lure of the North is still
irresistible in this exciting account of a fabled era of Canadian history.

Visit www.heritagehouse.ca to see the entire list of books in this series.

More Great Books in the Amazing Stories Series

Ghost Town Stories of BC

Tales of Hope, Heroism and Tragedy

(ISBN 978-1-894974-73-8)

Ghost Town Stories of Alberta

Abandoned Dreams in the Shadows of the
Canadian Rockies

(ISBN 978-1-894974-72-1)

Today, many of the historic mining communities of BC and the Alberta
Rocky Mountains are uninhabited ghost towns, disappearing into the
wilderness. Yet behind the crumbled ruins are tales of perseverance,
danger and romance. Johnnie Bachusky delves into pioneer history
in these two fascinating books that tell the dramatic and entertaining
stories of these vanished towns.

Visit www.heritagehouse.ca to see the entire list of books in this series.

More Great Books in the Amazing Stories Series

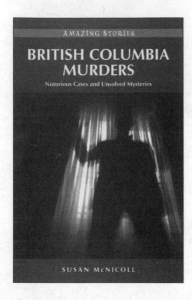

British Columbia Murders

Notorious Cases and Unsolved Mysteries

Susan McNicoll

(ISBN 978-1-926613-30-7)

In July 1924, Scottish nursemaid Janet Smith was murdered in Vancouver's wealthy Shaughnessy Heights. Her killer was never apprehended, but the investigation had shocking consequences. Twenty years later, Molly Justice was stabbed to death in a Saanich park. Her murderer has never been charged, even though police were virtually certain of his identity for over 50 years. Susan Nicoll's dramatic accounts of six of British Columbia's most intriguing murders span a century of crime, from a 1904 Victoria Chinatown murder to a modern cold case from Vernon solved through DNA analysis of an unusual kind.

Visit www.heritagehouse.ca to see the entire list of books in this series.